THE TEMPLE

OF CONSCIOUSNESS

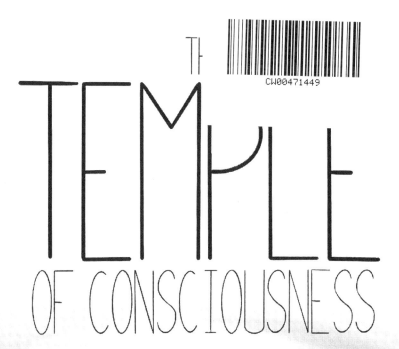

BROTHER

NOAH AGROTES

WELCOME TO THE NEW FUNDAMENTAL LIFE
AND THE EVOLUTIONARY WAY

The Temple of Consciousness, Noah Agrotes

ISBN: 978-9925-7764-0-5

www.thetempleofconsciousness.com

noahagrotes@yahoo.com

DEDICATION

To Joti, the light of the world...

CONTENTS

INTRODUCTION

At one point in my life, I realised that there was a serious and significant distinction between myself and the rest of the animals in the human zoo. On the journey of understanding my own diversity, I experienced extremely violent and painful experiences. Then, internally and spontaneously, an understanding emerged through the Spontaneous Forces in the universe that my brain is enhanced by the very rare properties of human DNA.

Inevitably, I turned my interest to the area of "elsewhere" and began my search for the eternal depths of the oceans of the universe, and all of the universes. You see, I have always ruled out the possibility that this life is the final stop on the journey. Thus, I found myself driving across the spiritual horizon of events towards the *ultimate* destination: becoming part of the cosmic plan that governs the lives of all humans and all living things in mortal realms similar to our Earth.

As I searched more, I began to realise that we live in a huge and fascinating capsular illusion created by Supreme Beings, who are much higher forms of intelligence and consciousness than us. A responsibility emerged to discover these Supreme Beings, our true leaders. Not from a desire for revenge or backlash against them, but with sentiments of peace and harmony towards them.

On this journey, I rejected the established models of understanding about human life. I decided definitively that I was detached from all animals and all human animals. In full harmony with the principles of logic, I sent an invitation to the Supreme Beings to settle in my human brain. The postman of this invitation was the Spontaneous Forces alive in the universe. The method of conveying the message was a spiritual wormhole, through which our natural laws can be bypassed. (If these concepts sound alien to you, fear not because you will learn how to harness them in this book.)

Time passed, and I experienced more violent and painful experiences, yet no acceptance of my invitation arrived. If you have ever suffered from mental turmoil, you will know that the violent experiences of an inner upheaval are infinitely more painful than physical, bodily experiences. However, this period of sacrifice turned out to be essential to my personal development. As I waited, I continued my daily life, communicating with people about business plans and activities, but I always kept in mind my strong desire to become the messenger of the Supreme Beings.

I had to wait a staggering 25 Earth years for my wish to come true—for the first settler to arrive. Those years were filled with violent conflicts and trials, which involved the most painful internal experiences. Yet, it was an indispensable period, as it enabled me to practice the acquirement of spiritual capabilities. It allowed me to integrate patience and persistence into my mindset. And due to the painful circumstances, it challenged me to the highest degree of difficulty, which is necessary for progress. Thanks to this period, I emerged as a brand-new self with multiple properties.

Thus, I welcomed, hosted, and became one with the Supreme Beings, 12 different colonists in the space of 6 years. My brain turned into a "hangout" for higher levels of consciousness, and the fact is that I love spending time there. As a result, I have left behind all established models of the Earth, freely travelling the galaxies in my spiritual pursuits and aspirations.

These colonists showed me the way—the evolutionary way—to the New Fundamental Life. Now, I am here to show you, dear reader, that same way.

Welcome to the New Fundamental Life

In this book, *The Temple of Consciousness*, you will come to understand the Supreme Beings and the new self. For now, it is important to understand that the Earth is of great value to the Supreme Beings, as it is an essential training school for consciousness. On this Earth, we must learn difficult lessons at the highest level of complexity if we want to evolve.

To succeed, and join the evolutionary way, there are five fundamental principles to live your life by. When you live these principles, you enter the area of the New Fundamental Life. These principles enable you to harness the Spontaneous Forces in the universe, which are the forces—or powers if you will—of the conscious realms of the universe applied here on Earth. The conscious realms are home to the Supreme Beings, the glorious Society of Composers, and the Temple of Consciousness.

As you traverse the New Fundamental Life, you will gain trophies. These trophies are shared among the victors, and they are unified time, collective observation, bodily intelligence, neutralisation, and freedom from the bonds of time and death. Yet, always keep in mind that your percentage of shares in these trophies will be very small as a beginner practicing the New Fundamental Life. On this path, I will teach you—not as a normal teacher but as a shareholder of the Spontaneous Forces and trophies of the universe.

I will teach you the five fundamental principles and their binding glue—patience. Patience is the connective tissue of all of the fundamental principles. Patience is pervasive in all of my teachings. Nothing is valid unless it is bound by the iron rod of patience. Sometimes, the spiritual mastery of patience for an individual will exceed the bounds of the mortal realm, and you may need to be patient for the space of two or three universes, but the spoils of victory are undoubtedly worth the wait.

This is the main equation of the Temple:

$$\text{Fundamental Principles} + \text{Spontaneous Forces}$$
$$= \text{Evolutionary Way} + \text{Trophies}$$

Is all of this shocking to you? As you will see in this book, the nature of consciousness means that we are all extra-terrestrials, even if we fail to understand that. In fact, there are many things that we fail to understand. If we follow the pattern of the universe and listen to approximate scientific measurements, more than 95% of the universe consists of dark matter and dark energy. Known visible matter occupies less than 5% of the whole universe. Thus, it is no surprise that we fail to grasp the true nature of consciousness, of life.

We fail to see that the Supreme Beings existed "elsewhere" long before the creation of the Earth, the solar system, the galaxy, and the universe. They exist *independently* of the universe. When I learned this, I rejected all of the anthropic principles, the models and theories of the nature of consciousness and cosmology, and the fallacies of scientists. I saw the true nature of things. As will you.

Thus, you will find that this book is a train full of surprises. One surprise will succeed the other until you reach the point of realisation that your life before this book was conducted with a lack of consciousness. And you will see the new way, the evolutionary way. But be patient with yourself. In this book, I am trying to describe the indescribable! I am seeking to describe what has not yet been described. Therefore, you are trying to understand the indescribable, and it will take time to comprehend and apply.

A warning for humanity

On your journey, you must watch out, because there are dangers afoot. While there are Supreme Beings that you may welcome into your brain, there are also Dark Rooms whose tenants will try to suck you into their abyss—the destruction of the Earth. The tenants of these Dark Rooms possess the world's wealth, and they are pushing the Earth to the brink of collapse through politics, the economy, democracy, and crime (issues that you will better understand through this book). Yet, those in the Dark Rooms can only lose in this game of self-destruction. Of course, billions of people on Earth will also lose. But what does he lose who has nothing to lose?

The Supreme Beings follow the developments on Earth with a neutral emotional load, but at the same time, they intervene with a positive spirit whenever required. If self-destruction does occur, the Supreme Beings will simply record the result and continue their work elsewhere.

We do not have much time left. The hourglass empties. We must change our course and preserve the Earth as a planet capable of hosting intelligent life or be dragged into everlasting destruction. Being honest, the odds are overwhelmingly against us. This mortal realm will eventually be destroyed by the greed of the tenants of the

Dark Rooms and the spiritual misery of their subjects—the people of the world.

Why? Because of the monumental absence of vision among the subjects who are untrained in the Fundamental Principles, and the inability of competent institutions to create a mentality of public interest rather than private interest. Thankfully, this book will teach you those Fundamental Principles, giving you a chance at escaping humankind's fate by entering the conscious realms.

No battle is lost beforehand! If that were the case, I wouldn't be here writing. If humans stop to reconsider the structural changes required in the whole spectrum of governance and the management of resources on this planet, then we might yet pop some bottles of champagne.

It's important to note that this book may come across as controversial and shocking. It contains ideas that you have probably never heard before. Despite this, they are not conspiracy theories. The events and scenarios I write about are already happening or will happen according to my prediction models, which are built on logical observation and the advanced form of bottom-up learning, which you will learn about in this book. To welcome the Supreme Beings, you must enter this book with an open mind.

I invite you, dear reader, to read this book carefully and lovingly. I invite you to love it! Here, I introduce to you a new sense of love. Love means passion to learn, passion to gain new power. It means knowledge, passion, and enthusiasm to abolish the old and adopt the new. It is passion to evolve and always move forward—never backwards.

While reading, remind yourself of your humility and kindness, as it may turn out to be the best thing in your life. And at some point, you may feel that the time has come to re-invent your own beliefs and attitude towards the established powers of authority, to what you have previously known. To enter the new evolutionary way, live the New Fundamental Life, and begin your journey to the Temple of Consciousness.

With that, let the reading begin!

.

PART 1

THE WORLD WE LIVE IN

Chapter 1

YOUR JOURNEY BEGINS

Your journey through life so far, your past, has led you here to this book. Your journey moving forward, your future, can be one of spiritual experiences and a connection to higher powers, or forces. But before you can harness these forces, you must understand what led you to where you are now and the key things that have shaped you on your journey.

You develop consciousness

At the moment of your birth, you know nothing. You arrive here on Earth with a unique supply of genetic cargo and the collective memories of the species you belong to. This collective memory drives the automatic, mechanical functions of your body and is embedded in what is known as the subconscious—just like every other species on Earth.

Do you understand that when you were born, you did not know anything and were like every other animal at the time of its birth? Your differentiation from the rest of the planet's animals begins when the burden of consciousness is stimulated in your brain.

Yet, the nature of human consciousness is not truly known to science. Scientists see consciousness as awareness of the self, the body, and the world around us. Some scientists estimate that we develop this consciousness very early in life, in our first twelve to fifteen months. Others suggest that new-born babies display a basic consciousness.[1]

According to science, we have only one nature as human beings: the material nature of cells, which are blocks of atoms of carbon, oxygen, hydrogen, nitrogen, calcium, phosphorus, and some others. Atoms are composed of particles such as protons, neutrons, and electrons. So to science, we are all children of the universe because we are all made from the same material or matter that was created in the various phases of life in the known universe over billions of years.

In mainstream science, this is the foundation of the anthropic principle. Accordingly, the material universe is composed of galaxies, stars, solar systems, and rock planets like Earth that develop life and intelligent life. The anthropic laws that stem from the anthropic principle allow the evolution of the species through natural selection.

My argument is that we have two natures, not one. Yes, our body has this material nature. But it also has a second nature: the nature of consciousness. I argue that consciousness is implanted in us after birth. In other words, we are not born with consciousness, nor do we develop it. This consciousness does not originate in the current material universe and does not belong to the matter of the material, known universe. Instead, it arrives in our brains as a colonist from the conscious, evolved universe, as you will learn in this book.

A brief history of consciousness

The Earth is around 4.5 billion years old. Throughout that time, intelligent life has occupied a very small part of it. Humans are estimated to have existed for around 6 million years, but these humans were not intelligent life and almost nothing like the humans we see today.[2] According to archaeologists, an estimated 200–300,000 years ago, humans became the Homo sapiens species, who we still call "modern humans".

At some point in the history of modern humans, Homo sapiens developed language. Scientists cannot agree on the reason why this occurred.[3] I argue that at this time, those in the conscious realms decided to colonise humans' minds with the capacity for consciousness—and the implantation of consciousness was the reason why humans were able to develop language after millions of years of silence and grunting like our fellow animals. We cannot know why our own animal was chosen and not another. We also cannot know whether other animals were chosen for this role elsewhere.

The burden of consciousness, the spark implanted in humans, only began to evolve in the last 10–12,000 years, which led modern humans to develop the first primitive foundations of civilisation. This led to the societies and humans we see around us today. But keep in mind that this intelligent evolution was not uniform. It did not involve the overwhelming majority of humans, who remained stagnant and extremely close to animals despite having villages, towns, and eventually sky-scraping cities.

Indeed, the evolution of consciousness is an extremely slow process. Does this surprise you? Just think, if I had been born 100 years ago, it would have been impossible for me to write this book. In fact, it would have been impossible to write this book 50, 30, or even 5 years ago!

In the human period of 6 million years of existence, it only became possible to write such a book in 2020. The preceding period was utterly inhospitable to advanced levels of consciousness and perception. This is happening for the first time in human history.

The anthropic and the non-anthropic

So we have a pair of natures, as we have a pair of universes: the material universe that we know and can observe—and an evolved universe that we do not know and cannot observe. As human bodies and brains, we are governed by the anthropic laws of the material universe, but as consciousness-load-carriers, we also have a non-anthropic nature.

Initially, the consciousness implanted in us is like a spark; it is minuscule in scope. But it has the capacity for explosive growth and endless expansion. In this way, we can understand that consciousness *is* awareness of the self, the body, and the universe around us, but with the capacity for unlimited forward expansion. This means that our consciousness can evolve and develop in many dimensions and more importantly, everywhere, and elsewhere forwards forever. It is infinite. This is true evolution.

Unfortunately, in most humans, it does not develop far beyond this initial spark, much less infinitely. This is why you may meet an old friend after 10 years and find they are exactly the same as they were a decade ago. In this book, you will discover how to expand your consciousness to join the evolutionary way. As yet, this hypothesis is unprecedented and unexplored. It has neither been researched nor studied by anyone in the history of Homo sapiens, until now.

Of course, scientists would laugh off such a hypothesis or similar radical ideas, and mainstream science would reject this theory before even genuinely considering it—without having any reasons to reject it. This is because mainstream science, contrary to what it conveys, takes an ideological approach. It only ever considers part of the picture.

The modern scientific understanding of the anthropic principle was suggested by Brandon Carter in 1973. It argues that:

1. Our existence in the universe necessarily is compatible with our existence within it as observers. (The weak anthropic principle)
2. The universe and the fundamental parameters that it depends on must be the way they are to allow the creation of observers within it (us). (The strong anthropic principle)

Within these two basic principles, a plethora of different versions are suggested by many scientists. Later, you will read my own version, which is the only logical one.

In other words, we exist within this universe, and it has the fundamental parameters, constants, and laws that it has. Our existence is evidence that the universe allows beings like us to exist within it. However, both the weak and strong anthropic principles are not widely accepted by scientists. Some famous Nobel prize winners reject them as nonsense, claiming that many illogical arguments have developed from them.

Personally, I accept these principles and expand them into new areas. But I reject any scientific approach that is not substantiated by the mother of all laws—logic—and so my arguments are always based on and governed by the logical principles. By contrast, some of the accepted scientific cosmological theories in our world are fundamentally devoid of logic and so deserve our total contempt and scorn (you will see some of these theories later).

The contribution of the material universe is magnificent and crucial. It gives you qualities that are primitive and unquestionable. You are what you are because of the universe—as a broad gathering of fundamental laws or as a function of all fundamental laws—and this determines your fate and destiny.

Look, friend, you are a carrier of genetic traits that define you as an Earthling, as the anthropic principle dictates. These qualities are very important. You can neither ignore them nor cancel them. In other words, you cannot be anything other than that. You cannot come from nowhere. You cannot submit to zero while you are proven to be part of one. There is no nothing, no zero. In a monumental and shocking clash between the material universe and the conscious realm, your properties were definitively and irreversibly determined. Your eternal process of birth and expansion was established.

You must always have in mind your natural origin, which is the origin of the universe. You must understand that like the universe, you were born spontaneously everywhere and not somewhere, and that you are expanding elsewhere forever.

The former means that the universe was born spontaneously everywhere—and not somewhere—because before genesis, there was a space-less situation, meaning there was no space to locate the point of the genesis of the material universe. Since then, it has been expanding elsewhere and forever, which means that *you* are evolving forever until you are reborn as a Supreme Being. You must understand that the Spontaneous Forces are the dominant form of power and law in the universe, and that because of them, you exist and can become a shareholder and member.

(We will further explore the marvellous, complex nature of consciousness and all the histories that arise from it in chapter 6.)

Within our material universe, there is only one planet known to host life, and that is our planet, Earth. On our planet, and every planet, the vital ingredient for life is water. Although astronomers have not yet determined whether there is life on other planets in our material universe, they do have criteria for locating such life and finding potentially habitable other planets.

Part of this criteria is that such planets must have similar qualities to Earth, for example, water in liquid form. For other planets in our material universe, their orbit must not be too close or too far from a star to maintain liquid water. If it were, then the water would either boil or freeze. Thus, astronomers developed the so-called "Goldilocks Zone" to define the habitable range for water in liquid form to exist on a planet's surface, conditions where it is not too hot nor too cold for life to exist, but just right. Astronomers have made discoveries in the Goldilocks Zone, for example, an Earth-size planet called Kepler-186f. One day, they hope that such discoveries will lead us to water and therefore life.

Thus, the universal law of our universe is that nothing is viable unless it is fair. This is my law. The Goldilocks Zone is astronomers' description of the applied circumstances of a viable planet. My law, the universal law of fairness, is the transportation of those conditions after the appearance of intelligent life. The Goldilocks zone is "the before"—meaning what happened for us to be here on this planet. Life is possible because of the water-in-liquid-form state.

My law is the after, the now. Now, life is an event on planet Earth. To remain in existence, life must occur in fair conditions. These fair conditions have nothing to do with this book. With or without this book, the conditions must be fair, otherwise no life will continue to exist, and as for human species, no civilisation will continue to exist. Life must be just right—just fair.

The prison of life

Though you were born ignorant, your family, school, and nation begin to mould you and integrate you into society. These are the agents of your primary development. From a young age, you also join circles of friends in your school and neighbourhood, and maybe a host of virtual "friends" on the internet.

Then, those with authority take control of you. I am not referring to the government here. I am talking about the Dark Rooms, the people of authority in this world. You may have heard them called by a different name because many people are aware of their existence. A new group—the "digerati"—have established their own throne. Former U.S. Secretary of Foreign Affairs Colin Powell stated that no more than 500 supremely rich people or families control all of the power structures in the USA. This includes the Pentagon, the Department of State, the intelligence agencies, and the Federal Reserve Bank.

No matter who is elected President of the United States, these people and families hold the real power. Neither Donald Trump nor Joe Biden has any real power to do anything revolutionary if it will go against the interests of the rich families in control. Thus, the Dark Rooms are the true authorities in the world, while the elected politicians and governments are merely their puppets. Accordingly, a small group own, manage, and exploit more than 50% of the world's wealth. The remainder is split between the rest of the human population, which is thinly spread.

Beware. While you know nothing, the authorities know everything about you. Contrary to what most people believe, those in power are not interested in your personal identity, your name, or even your bank details. They are interested in more significant things. They are concerned with keeping you a lifelong captive, chaining you spiritually to serve them, and preventing you from living autonomously. In essence, they want you to become their servant, and that is the subject of their interest.

The methodology of the authorities is simple—to absolutely control your family, your school, your workplace, and your nation. Terrifying as it is to hear, your family are also captives, chained spiritually. The authorities allow you and your fellow humans to exist for one reason—to carry out their commands without resisting. This is why you and your family almost certainly do not feel like people trapped and deprived of their liberty. Instead, they conform with absolute conviction that it is the right thing to do. Moreover, it is a societal necessity!

The family

You are probably wondering "but how do the Dark Rooms infiltrate my life?" Well, it begins with your family. In Western society, certain patterns prevail, provided you are fortunate to be born into a typical, normal family that is integrated into the system of authority. However, if you are born into an excluded, marginalized, or economically challenged family, then your chances are limited. Not exactly zero, but you have a near-zero probability. You form part of "expendable humanity".

In this section, I will deal exclusively with the typical families of the West, although the number of non-integrated families is rising sharply and leaning toward those who are integrated. In fact, we have reached a point where there are no substantial differences between a great number of families, unlike the class divides of the past. (The subject of expendable humanity will be addressed in chapter 2.)

Your family is the first station for your education and ideas when you arrive on this planet. Therefore, a typical family is very strictly organised around a specific framework of education. You grow up in limited circumstances within your family. You learn by the top-down method, which means that your parents teach you what they know. They have the conviction that what they know is correct and the right thing for you to learn. But have you ever wondered whether your parents really know what is happening to them? Of course not. You are taught to "listen to your parents, listen to your teachers, listen to authority."

The system of knowledge that the authorities impose is top-down learning. Gradually, this method renders you unable to exercise your astonishing, latent ability to learn by the bottom-up method. This is the freedom to acquire knowledge and spiritual experiences through self-education. This way of acquiring knowledge and intellectual experiences is not promoted because the authorities seek full control over you for life. Self-learning and freedom—the natural choice— are forbidden fruits that they never want you to taste. Not only are you forbidden from tasting them, but you are forbidden from even believing that they exist! Your parents do not realise that they exist.

This is one of the reasons why titans of intelligence are no longer prevalent. The necessary conditions to develop new champions in this evolutionary race are no longer present. The evolutionary race of intelligence will be addressed in later chapters. For now, it's enough to acknowledge that the Homo sapiens species has ceased to evolve mentally, not because it has reached the exceptional conditions of mental perfection—that is far from the case—but because it has obligatorily been limited to a non-evolutionary state by the wealthy authorities, who prevent any kind of development.

In the last 10 years, there has been abundant evidence of a disorderly regression—if you look around you and are old enough to make the comparison, of course. This regression can be seen in the people you meet every day. There are obvious indications and signs everywhere that we are in a decaying world society, as so many human behaviours centre around anger, disgust, and aversion. (These capacities and mentalities are bad for you, but they can be applied as strong assets when you become a mystic of neutralisation, as you will learn later.)

As we grow up, we often learn these abhorrent behaviours from our family, from our parents in particular. We witness their hatred, and so we hate too. We take on their disgusts and aversions to certain things, people, and places. We are carbon copies of them, and so the system infiltrates our minds.

The journey of education

At some point on your path through life, you go to school. Even if your parents were careful not to pass their negative behaviours on to you, they cannot control every environment you are in. Thus, you learn these harmful behaviours at school—from your friends, your enemies, and even your supposed teachers.

At school, your mind is clouded over by the unnecessary knowledge of top-down learning. You are taught nonsense such as algebra that will not help you in your basic human life, let alone to evolve. You are also required to participate in a system of developing technical skills so you can go to university and specialise in these skills. In this way, you are prepared for the so-called "labour market". If you are not prepared and equipped with the necessary skills, you will be— as the media skilfully threatens you—out of the labour market and forced to succumb to unemployment.

The school, as an arm of the authorities, is not interested in shaping you into a thoughtful and logical person. Its aim is to convert you into a consumable resource to be expended in the labour market as a useful idiot. Schools do not attempt to guide you through life, and towards evolvement, by teaching you to educate and develop yourself. On the contrary, they direct you to become an unthinking tool with a very limited perception of space and consciousness so you can be controlled forever. In short, spiritual or mental autonomy is not permissible.

During your formative years, you attend speeches and all manner of seminars and lessons from "teachers". All of these speakers portray themselves as wise experts who want to convince you of your future success. Everyone is interested in you! But the only thing of *real* interest to them is the money they are paid to be there. Whether they are your parents, state institutions, or private professional organisers of seminars and lectures, they are selling you false dreams, non-existent successes, falsely magnified reputations, and shallow glory.

Everyone talks to you about innovation, entrepreneurship, and new ideas that will revolutionise the market and ensure a prosperous future for you. Yet, they cunningly conceal the reality of the economy and the nature of the structures that govern and sustain it. This reality can be summarised in a simple statement—"There is no room for you. All seats are reserved."

No matter what you do, how specialised you become, and how creative and innovative you are, your dream will always be just out of reach. You will always have just missed it. Your investment will always have been just lost. But the economy will continue to churn, no matter who wins and loses. The economy has no need for you, your innovative ideas, your ingenuity, or even your boundless energy. There will always be someone else to take your place.

Despite this, there are speakers who try to encourage you to multiply, unceasingly introducing new methodologies to immerse you in your illusory future success. Ignore them. They have nothing to tell you and nothing useful to teach you. You are wasting your time and money by putting your faith in modern-day soothsayers of your non-existent future success. Stop paying them.

Watch out, because the speakers from organised religions, while not suggesting financial methodologies to you, can also seek to retain you as resources for their religion and their ideology. Please note that, in this book, I do not argue for or against any particular religion. I simultaneously respect and reject all religions. I keep some precious, inspired teachings for myself from great teachers such as the Prophet Muhammad (PBUH), Buddha, Confucius, Jesus of Nazareth, Thales of Miletus, Socrates, Plato, Leonardo Da Vinci,

Michelangelo, Galileo, Newton, Einstein, Dirac, and the Ancient Egyptian Pharaohs.

However, I retain only *some* of their teachings, because as humans, they were all vulnerable to false conclusions and becoming trapped in their mistakes. This is our nature—to make mistakes every day, among other capacities of course.

All of these people and their ideas shaped humanity so much that their life stories became shrouded in myths and legends. There are many fantastical stories told about their lives, but I am sceptical of many of these stories because we have no evidence for their veracity. I believe that we should focus on the inspired *teachings* of these people rather than the supernatural stories told about their lives. A teacher is one thing; a religion based on specific teachings is a whole other thing.

The slavery of the suit

While you spend your time trying to "get rich quick" or fight someone else's war (physical or religious), you are distracted from the reality of your everyday life and the truth of your job. The 21st century's form of slavery is the job, the occupation. Indeed, modern slaves now walk around in a suit and tie. All of these beings in suits are so satisfied with their personal lives that they define what we perceive as happiness! A stable job, a nice house, a shiny car, a few holidays each year, and 2.4 children. Is that not our 21st century definition of happiness, or some variation of it?

Yet, this is merely an example of shallowness in our perception and consciousness. The directed life, which consists of a specific way of functioning and acting, is the result of imposition. That is what they want for you. The invisible authorities have trapped you in this minuscule life. They have defined the space in which you can move and act. They have trapped you in this space, and the keys are in the possession and control of the privileged few.

Thus, you are a prisoner of your environment and circumstances— your family, school, friends, workplace, and nation. You grew up in this enclosed space without the ability to explore, without the ability to question whether things could be different from how you were trained to experience them, and without any perception of the other dimensions of space where intellectual freedom and freedom of choice might prevail through natural selection.

You become a fish who swims around in a glass tank and gladly declares itself happy. Go and observe a fish as it swims, then place yourself in its position. You see yourself as above the fish, as far superior. But in reality, you do not differ by much. The fish has its tank and cannot go any further because it is ignorant of anything beyond its immediate surroundings. Thus, its happiness is complete.

In the same manner, your happiness is complete as you carry out the will of the authorities. You cannot go further into other areas of perception and consciousness because you are unaware of their existence. The authorities have programmed you to declare yourself happy and create other happy people like yourself, who are called "offspring" and who continue in the same process of creating happiness. In this way, the wealthy authorities of the world become increasingly entrenched and consolidated in society.

The Dark Rooms

Unfortunately, through their actions, those in the Dark Rooms are unknowingly and unwittingly driving the potential intelligent life of this planet to extinction. What they fail to realise is that they will face severe losses through their actions. Therefore, their indifference and ignorance towards the consequences of their actions are misguided. It is a case of incorrectly judging the effects of one's actions.

Their dominion and power over the planet cannot continue when there are no inhabitants. Who will they rule over when everyone disappears? How long will the food and water reserves last in their underground shelters? What will they do with their time when they are deprived of their favourite hobbies: money and luxuries?

Those in power will simply live a little longer than common mortals, but they will live like condemned mice hiding underground. There will be no trace of hope that the former state of affairs will return, with its prestige, wealth, and prosperity. The most likely scenario is that they will commit suicide or starve one after another until not one survivor of the disaster remains.

They live in an enormous bubble of illusion. Luxury, opulence, and wealth exist only in comparison to people who are deprived of basic needs, and thus these things cannot exist in isolation. Imagine a situation where the deprived classes cease to exist. To whom will the rich gloat? Where will they extract natural resources from when all of the resources are exhausted?

To understand how this coexistence works, consider this: the best tennis players in the world are recognised as such because of the world rankings. To reach this pinnacle, they have to beat the rest of the players in scheduled tournaments. They cannot be the best by remaining self-contained and isolated. They must coexist with others, play against them, and beat them. In the same manner, self-sufficient wealth cannot exist without others to produce this wealth on their behalf.

You would be forgiven for seeing this as a depressing situation. However, at least one person may have realised what will happen in the forthcoming disaster. There is at least one tenant in the Dark Rooms who can sound the alarm. Not just one, but plenty. There are many who worry about the consequences without knowing how to force a change.

Some may believe that these events will lead to disaster but one that will only affect later generations. Thus, they remain inactive in the lethargy of delusion. They fail to realise that this self-destruction *will* affect them. They believe that the disaster will not happen soon, will not affect their lives or the lives of their children or grandchildren.

Their main hypothesis, supported by scientists, is that we will somehow find a way to escape to another planet 100 or 200 years from now. My strong belief, due to the physical nature of the human body, is that it is impossible to escape to another planet, not in 100 or 200 years. Not ever. And besides, how can we escape in 100 or 200 years if nobody is left here to escape?

We can only hope that someone sounds the alarm before it is too late and that we can stop our planet from being destroyed.

The first step

For now, the first step of your personal revolution is seeing things as they truly are. Recognising your life as a prison that you have been confined to by those in control. However, a single revolutionary step is not enough. Many steps, many struggles, and colossal effort will be necessary on this journey. To proceed, you need to know the five fundamental principles, so fasten your seatbelt and let us enter the evolutionary way.

Chapter 2

THE FIVE FACTORS OF EXPENDABLE HUMANITY

Les Miserables, expendable humanity. Although your future is extremely gloomy, I do not wish to be the Cassandra of Calamity. I merely look around me and make sensible conclusions based on what I see. Rare and unprecedented factors that have never occurred in economic history are surfacing now. Never before in the productive history of Homo sapiens' activities have we witnessed such a terrible combination of factors. So, before you proceed on your journey to evolution, it is important to understand and successfully navigate the mortal realm you are living in.

The five factors that are colliding in the early 21st century are as follows:

1. Growth of the global population.
2. Migration as a result of the "better life" illusion.
3. Elastic employment and wage squeezing.
4. Business globalisation from rapid technological development.
5. The hyper-concentration of wealth.

In this chapter, I will analyse the dangerous combination we are facing and what it means for the planet and its inhabitants.

1. Growth of the global population

Today, the population of the planet has exceeded 7.5 billion people. We humans are not the masters of the cosmic plans for the universe, so we should not judge this fact, and I am not judging; I am simply quoting numbers. I do not regard every new birth as a bothersome new unit, nor do I consider every new arrival a fool to be exploited like the conspirators in the Dark Rooms do.

However, all of the economic theories of the past were built on the notion that there is room for everyone to contribute to the production process while consuming what is necessary for them to survive. These theories suggest that there is scope for a perpetual process of exchange, where the employee offers their work and the capitalist offers a monetary reward in return—a salary—so the entire exchange system operates to the optimal degree.

Unfortunately, none of the thinkers of economic theories took note of the factors that would invalidate the structure of their theories, such as the future overpopulation of the planet. This overpopulation is in the context of its interaction with the other four factors. If only one or two of these factors were occurring, there would be no overcrowding. The maximum potential of this planet to sustain the population is far larger than today's number of inhabitants. However, these possibilities have been razed to the ground due to the five factors intermingling.

What is more, the rapid growth of the human population is primarily occurring in specific places, particularly in underprivileged countries. It is estimated that 97% of human population growth by 2030 will occur in developing countries.[4] At the same time, the area of land available for production per capita is dramatically reducing. In other words, these countries are being filled to the point of strangulation.

Moreover, the environment in these countries can be fierce and even violent. The conditions that are favourable for the development of intelligent life often do not exist there. If we are being honest with ourselves in our supposedly comfortable Western lifestyles, not only do we *not* see any improvement in the standard of living in these countries, but we can even observe their continuous degradation toward being an inhospitable environment.

Unfortunately, those in the Dark Rooms have decided that it will be this way, and these countries do not have room to breathe life into their economies for the sake of their inhabitants. Because of this, the developing world is not governed by any of our former economic theories. It does not obey economic axioms.

2. Migration as a result of the "better life" illusion

As a result of the first factor, new generations in developing countries are trapped in figurative cages. They know there are well-paid jobs overseas in the West, where they could make their dreams a reality. Thus, the Western world becomes a Promised Land for people seeking a better quality of life. However, it means leaving their home, and make no mistake, this often means abandoning a beautiful and paradisiacal landscape that nobody would ordinarily want to leave.

Those seeking a new life in the West may apply for so-called "political asylum", but in reality, they may simply be looking for a well-paying job, which is something they cannot secure in their home country. If they do find a well-paying job, it may be in harsh or violent conditions that are out of balance with the process of exchange.

As a result, the young generations in underprivileged countries invent feasible and infeasible methods of escape. Their desperate attempts to reach the Promised Land are even shown on television. Since the proposed reward is a better life, they are willing to juggle the element of danger. You can see human beings stacked on top of each other, crossing seas and rivers on dangerous modes of transport, passing through war zones, and climbing high walls—all for the prize of a better life.

Nothing can erase or destroy the dreams of people in underprivileged countries. Why, you ask? It is because they know they are being wronged! They know they deserve a better life like their counterparts in privileged countries. This is why they plan their voyage of escape— their journey of freedom. But does what they are dreaming of *really* exist? Is there a "better life" out there? Or is it another illusion that exists exclusively in the minds of the desperate?

I have a 23-year-old Indian housekeeper named Joti, and because of her, I love India and feel a deep connection with Indian people. Joti sought out a livelihood so far away from her home country to help her brother study and to contribute to her father's medical treatment. She says she is happy with me and tells her family this every day.

She has an income—set by the law—which is dreamlike by her country's standards but very small by the Western world's standards. Maybe she is lucky that she found me, and I am lucky to have found her. However, she could have done so much more with her life if this terrible imbalance of economic exchange did not exist in her great country, just like the other developing countries and emerging economies. She could be with her own family, in her home country. This is why the "better life" is an illusion.

Meanwhile, as waves of people are preparing for, or even making, their exodus to the Promised Land, the Western governments are asleep as usual, or so busy engaging in corrupt activities that they have no time to deal with such serious issues. They are too busy looking after their own interests.

It is like we are on an unpiloted ship in the middle of the ocean, which is being governed by a chaotic autopilot program experiencing technical difficulties. Meanwhile, castaways from other ships are trying to board ours. As a result, the unpiloted, overloaded ship is headed toward the rocks, where it will deliver all of its passengers into the cold hands of death. Truly, how many castaways can we save from the shipwreck that is the global economy?

Please note that I am not judging the people who arrive daily by every imaginable method; I am not worthy of judging anyone. It is the present system of global power that I judge, which has pushed much of the world's population further into poverty. Pushed them to the point where they must seek a basic survival elsewhere.

Maybe one day, the people who are living in wait of an escape will be able to find success in their own countries, which are far more beautiful than ours. Maybe these countries will be able to harness their productive potential and view the West as an example of what not to do, rather than the Promised Land.

3. Elastic employment and wage squeezing

Across the Western world, in both Europe and America, there is a rise in unemployment. While the media suggest that unemployment is reducing, what we are actually seeing is the "elasticity" of employment. This is where millions of people work part time, a few hours per week, or on "zero hours" contracts, yet are considered "employed" according to the official figures.

This elastic employment is replacing traditional forms of employment, but in reality, it is simply a new form of *un*employment. The young and upcoming generations suffer the most from it, and it should be a matter of great concern to us because there is no realistic hope that these young people will experience better working conditions in the future.

At some point, there will be no difference between the employed and the unemployed because "wages" in the elastic employment model will fall to the same level as unemployment benefits. In fact, this is already happening and it is just a matter of time before it becomes cataclysmic. Eventually, we will arrive at the depressing state where many people will be both employed and unemployed at the same time. That is to say, they will be considered "employed" by statistical measurements but will be on the same income footing as those registered as unemployed.

Unfortunately, immigrants inadvertently contribute to the proliferation of this phenomenon since they accept work for very low wages, deceived by the illusion that what they receive is a rather high wage. Indeed, it is perhaps 10 or 20 times greater than what they would have received in their home country, but it is still a low wage. (Note that I am not judging them for this choice but the system that makes this a necessity.)

Western economists argue that immigration develops the economy of the host country, and this is partly correct. This development occurs because wages are constantly being squeezed and lowered. With this sophisticated method in place, the international competitiveness of Western countries towards the giants of Asia is gratified.

However, the logical consequence is a deterioration in the overall quality of life in Western countries. Hence, any growth is merely a bubble. In the long term, it fails to deliver benefits to the standard of living for people in that country. On the contrary, we can watch any statistical and development of figures on paper go hand in hand with the decline of citizens' actual quality of life.

4. Business globalisation from rapid technological development

In business, globalisation means "companies operating across the globe to produce goods or services." Although this process is driven by trade and investment, it is hugely enabled by technology and computers. Today, every human being as a unit of activity can produce far more in a much shorter amount of time than in the past due to revolutionary technology and computers.

In fact, the unit of activity has grown to such unprecedented levels that one person can do as much work in a day as would have required the cooperation of thousands of people in the past. As an example, there is more Tabasco sauce made in one day now for global consumption than its creator Edmund McIlhenny made in his entire life.[5]

Unfortunately for humankind, giant technological companies and the big industrial forces of the Western world have exploited this productivity by expanding into other areas of the world to gain cheap labour. In the process, such companies seize the technological power of these countries and harvest their productive resources, that is, anyone who may produce goods. Of course, this is for the good of the company, not for the good of the local inhabitants. Not for the good of that country either, since its inhabitants are lining the pockets of Western countries and not their own.

I live in Cyprus, where I could run a very nice hotel with a personal approach to tourists. This would be the action of a productive resource. There are two players here: the individual and their country. The individual has potential productive capabilities depending on their personality, talents, passion, knowledge, experience, and personal funds (or borrowing, if they are comfortable with this). The country offers the individual their original investment ground—in the case of Cyprus, the sea, the sun, good food, a very low crime rate, and beautiful archaeological sites.

However, I could not succeed in such an enterprise because the international hotel chains own most of the hotels in Cyprus, and the big tour operators leave almost no room for small, independently owned hotels. In the tiny amount of room left for small businesses, they cannot charge what they deserve to earn because they are forced to compete on an uneven playing field. Instead, they are obliged to charge rates so low that in the long term, they often cannot survive against the competition.

In poor countries, the situation is even worse. The local population rarely have the option to practice their talents, nor the country to offer its natural bounties. Their productive resources are often consumed by these overseas giants. Thus, the local population live like slaves to foreign giants. With their pitifully low salaries as a result of business globalisation, they are forever poor, and their only dream —if they are young enough—is to move to a Western country for a potentially better chance at life. What a horrible reality we live in!

The seizing of productive resources through technological forces is a dangerous practice that undermines peace and security, not only in developing countries but across the entire globe. This process turns people into expendable humanity. As you can see, there are especially vulnerable groups for expendability among the world's population: the inhabitants of developing or emerging economies. But it is not only them who are at risk—you are also a candidate.

Even if you had the privilege of being born and raised in the West, your position is not set in stone, and you are not guaranteed freedom from expendability. Everyone in every country of the world, in every corner of the planet, is a possible candidate for the expendable humanity category. Nobody has the privilege of exemption, except those in the Dark Rooms, who hold the wealth and the power.

Those in the Dark Rooms mistakenly believe that the costs of this process will be borne by the hard-working citizens of Western countries. Over a few decades, those living in "rich" Western societies will be forced to work at increasingly lower wages compared to the cost of living. Eventually, the immigrants will be "integrated" into their new societies, only they will now be the societies of the world's poor.

If you think you are safe from this danger, think again. It will not be long before the arrival of people from developing countries puts pressure on you too. Every day, crowds of smart and creative people arrive from developing areas with skills and adaptability that are infinitely more developed than yours. You are not smarter than them. Never let that thought cross your mind, or you will lose the game.

On the contrary, these people are much more experienced at fighting for their survival than you are. Because of this, business globalisation confronts you with facts of life that you had never even considered before. From then on, you are forced to participate in the race for survival—not only as an individual but as a family, a society, and a nation.

Moreover, this race for survival involves elements that are entirely new to you. The main element is your obligation to revise and adapt the way you think and act. The system taught you that there was a standard of stability for you, that you were secure, and that there were enough jobs for everyone. Now you realise that standard is disappearing. Now, you are not safe, and you are not guaranteed a job. Instability is universal, even if some regions of the world are able to maintain local stability for a while. If you do not believe that the race for survival has already begun, then you are in the dark, my friend.

The conditions of this race are extremely complicated, and only a few will end up being the progenitors of a new generation of people with higher intelligence. (In fact, the race for survival is simultaneously the race to evolve into a new level of intelligence, which will be discussed in chapter 7).

No one decided it was time for the race for survival to be run; instead, the era demanded it. It emerged as a necessity caused by the conditions on this planet—the five factors—and it is being pushed to its limit by those who hold the wealth and power.

5. The hyper-concentration of wealth in the hands of a small group of people

Do not be fooled by the prosperity that is preserved in some parts of the population. Do not get carried away by the glittering luxury that is shown on your television screen. Only a very small percentage of the population actually live in such luxury. The vast majority of global citizens face serious difficulties as poverty and unemployment continue to blight humanity.

Consider that in 2019, global unemployment was 4.94%, which is 350 million people![6] With the Covid-19 pandemic, this unemployment figure has sky-rocketed, with an estimated 305 million full-time job equivalents lost in the second quarter of 2020 alone.[7]

If you are one of the fortunate people who live in a stable economy, have retained your job, and believe that everything is wonderful, consider your fellow humans who are less fortunate. Consider that 736 million people (8.6%) in the world live in *extreme* poverty. More than half of these live in sub-Saharan Africa. In the Middle East and North Africa, those living in extreme poverty have almost doubled in the past two years.[8]

A quarter of people in the world live without electricity. We live in a world where hunger due to poverty is still the biggest killer. And yet poverty is not just a problem in developing countries. It is important to realise that 39.7 million people (12.3%) live in poverty in the supposedly glittering USA.

Why is this the case when there is plenty of money, plenty of resources, for every human on earth? Well, it is widely known that the world's 26 richest people have more money than the world's poorest 50% *combined*.[9] We know that those in the Dark Rooms keep the wealth for themselves while letting the rest of humankind suffer, starve, and die.

What you must understand is that super rich people are *not* normal people. They are maniacs addicted to money and its power. If you search, you will easily find some super rich beasts, near or over the age of 90, whose only concern is how to increase their wealth. Every day, they fight to increase their fortune, and they live under the illusion that they are immortal! These beasts are enemies of humanity, and while I rate them as my enemies, they should be rated by everybody as enemies of intelligent life on planet Earth.

There are of course other super rich beasts who are younger and have a "philanthropy hobby", as I call it. Some of them are very well-known as philanthropists. However, this hobby does not make these people any less demonic. In fact, their philanthropy is outright hypocrisy. How the hell do these beasts sleep at night knowing that billions of people have not even got a piece of bread to eat, or have to fight to secure that piece of bread? This is a logical question. Unfortunately, such people are not governed by logic, only by their manic addiction to becoming even richer. In truth, they do not give a penny for what is happening outside their glass towers of wealth. Indeed, concern about expendable humanity is for us, not for them!

Some of those in the Dark Rooms are visible to all of us; others remain invisible forever. Regardless, the power of money rules the world in an extremely aggressive and violent way, no matter whether some of the Dark Rooms' residents come to the media with a smile and gentle behaviour. Theirs is the smile of a demon for sure.

The power of money is so tyrannic and so against humanity's essential life sources that every new day on this planet is worse than every yesterday. Over time, the planet will become more and more inhospitable for the development of intelligent life and indeed, inhospitable for any kind of life. So, while some members of the Dark Rooms may be visible to us as human figures, the power of money is invisible to the miserable rest of humanity.

However, we can take a different view on the owners of global wealth and the new properties that capital carries. Capital has neither borders nor currency. It has the property of constantly transforming into any kind of currency, in any area of globalisation and any market. Capital also has another property: the bigger it gets, the smaller it feels. The bigger it is, the more savage and inhuman it is. There are no limits to the misconduct of the capitalists of the Dark Rooms. There are no limits to their greed and obsession for expansion at the detriment of the productive resources—the people. I repeat, there is absolutely no limit.

You might wonder, "But what are they ultimately doing? Who do they think they are? What do they think will happen if they accumulate the whole of global production in their power? Don't they understand that they will wipe us out as a human species and that they will be eradicated with us?"

Sorry, friend, but there is no point in asking these logical questions. He who is addicted to heroin, gambling, or alcohol does not understand things on logical grounds. The same goes for someone addicted to the obsessive expansion of capital. Yes, being a member of the world's capitalist power is an extremely addictive emotion, which ends up being an addictive delusion. In this delusion, those in the Dark Rooms push us towards the path of self-destruction for our species.

The combination of the five factors

Though originally hospitable to life, we are making this planet inhospitable through our insane actions and our stubborn persistence in misanalysing the effects of our choices. For example, we are passionate about technological development and globalisation in business, but we give no consideration to its negative effects on people's ability to actually sustain their livelihoods.

Over time, the combination of these five factors will result in the creation of a new order of the world's poor, who will form the majority. Not just in developing countries, but everywhere. Thus, the citizens of Western societies will slowly but steadily become candidates for exodus themselves.

The majority of the world's population will turn into an amorphous mass of expendable people, becoming expendable humanity as the unavoidable result of these five factors combining. This means that a huge percentage of humanity will be rendered useless. Absolutely useless.

This is the present and the future for the poor of the world. There will be no space left for them to practice as productive resources of a surviving axiom anywhere in the world. The world is saying to them "Hey, don't even consider it; you are lost and useless forever." And being expendable humanity is the worst nightmare for logical, thinking, feeling people.

My model of the future based on the five factors and their combination predicts that citizens' wrath will wrongly turn toward the immigrants in their country. In the seemingly privileged countries, the citizens who see their income continuously decreasing compared to the cost of living—being plagued by unemployment—will look for someone to blame. As always, immigrants will be their target. You only have to look at the lack of integration of communities in America to see the truth of this.

In fact, it is easy to see how people's beliefs are shaped. A prolonged period of instability that causes unemployment and a decline in the standard of living pushes the masses to search for a "culprit". Then, when such a culprit is identified, they must be crucified—the masses do not have the necessary intellectual background to judge and draw conclusions from their actions.

As a result, societal peace and prosperity will be severely disrupted in the countries that are currently seen as privileged. Any so-called "integration" will fail, and it will provoke hugely explosive social outbursts. Wars or riots will break out in the cities of the West, where the poor will fight against the poor, the cursed against the cursed, the expendable against the expendable.

The political battleground

In this aggravated climate, various political scammers are hurrying to gain political and economic profit from the discontent among the masses. They artificially exacerbate the popular feeling of revenge and punishment against the culprit. The political rationales they proclaim are words of hate against these unfortunate people.

The masses form a prevalent set of common beliefs in every age, and politicians who wish to wage wars exploit this common belief for their own benefit. In our time, these prevalent beliefs will pit politicians against immigrants. Populist beliefs will legitimise violence, as they did in the past. However, they will fail to achieve anything other than chaos.

In Europe, there is a rift between the populists, as they are called, and the political establishment. The object of this dispute is the Euro and migrants. I believe that the defeat of the political establishment is certain, and that they will be overthrown by the populists. But either way, I urge you to stay far away from both as they are highly dangerous. Although they come from different places, they are both contributing to the destruction of Europe, whether they realise it or not.

I invite you to be on your guard. Dramatic developments will follow, notably in Europe where the theatre-of-war operations will take place precisely as they did in the two previous phases of the World War. We had World War 1 and World War 2. Now, Europe is the main theatre of battles for World War 3—although it is not a war of weapons this time.

The populists will be legitimised by the strong popular belief that immigrants are responsible for their suffering, and the collapse of the Eurozone will happen simultaneously due to the greed of banks. The banks and economies of the Eurozone countries will disappear, and chaos will emerge everywhere.

Conflicts between civilians and the police will occur daily, and civilian attacks against immigrants will multiply, taking the form of poor people revolting against other poor people, those who are suffering as much and sometimes more than they are.

The way out

If you're wondering "What should I do?", then the answer is this. I invite you to ignore the political establishment who are responsible for the globalisation of poverty and have no right to represent those who care about immigrants. Turn your back on the political establishment. Never forget that this establishment is the real culprit for your misfortune and misery because it carries out the instructions of the Dark Rooms like a puppet on strings. As for the populists, I invite you to ignore them too because their ideologies are the refuge of the fraudsters who plunder your life. It is not possible, nor useful, to support ideologies about who is responsible for the catastrophe.

However, I will emphasize it again: I am not against the people who are frantically seeking an exodus to the Promised Land. I am not against unhappy people. I stand with these people now, in these difficult times, and especially in the seasons to come. But I am not the authorities, and I cannot guarantee a stable and peaceful environment for them in the Promised Land.

Instead of misdirecting your wrath at these people, you have to stand tall and defend them with dignity. Immigrants are not your enemies; I hope you understand that. The fact that immigrants might take over your living space is a consequence of a lack of space for everyone to make a living. They are not coming to take your position; that is not their intention when they make their great escape. They come because they have no other place to survive in. Would you deny them the right to life?

No, my friend, your enemies are the titans of the Dark Rooms whose actions transform you from a human being into expendable humanity. Enlist your wisdom and pride. In the rough weather that will follow, stand up and extend a protective shield to your defenceless fellow men who are victims, as are you, of the extreme absurdity of the Dark Rooms. Defend each other until the end.

The end is nigh

According to the various scenarios envisioned by futurists and scientists, the end of the world might be caused by an asteroid impact, nuclear warfare, biological warfare, large-scale natural disasters, an alien invasion, or many other scenarios with varying dates and timescales.

However, I believe that our Armageddon is just around the corner, and that it will not come from an asteroid nor an alien invasion, since nobody in this universe gives a penny about us. We may have less than 30 years left to come to our senses. Perhaps 30 years is an optimistic prediction. I believe that we exceeded the limits of our potential for rescue and the bounds of this planet's hospitality long ago.

Thus, the time of the great turning point—the singularity—is approaching. Expendable humanity is the factor that will bring about the end of humankind. The end will spontaneously emerge as the result of an extremely incorrect analysis of the consequences of the flawed actions of those in the Dark Rooms. The degradation of the majority of people into expendable humanity will cause Armageddon if we are unable to turn the tide.

The end of the world has two different paths. One leads to the end of civilisation and the extinction of the human species. The other leads to the re-invention of life on this planet and the emergence of the winner of the intelligence race. This new form of intelligence will replace the failed, out-of-control Homo sapiens species (you will learn more about this evolutionary race in chapter 7).

Let us come to terms with the last days. We must urgently escape from all of the greediness of humankind. We do not have much time at our disposal, or we will be forever lost from the face of the Earth. Yet, success lies in our hands. We have before us a unique opportunity to move forward as humans.

Our message to the Dark Rooms

Finally, our goal as responsible people must be to persuade those in power to change the way in which they view the world. We must show them it is their own interests that are at stake. If the planet is destroyed, they will lose the most in the wreckage because they possess the most. What do the billions of expendable people have to lose? What can they lose who have nothing to lose?

We must encourage those in the Dark Rooms to read the consequences of their decisions correctly. They misanalyse the facts surrounding their decisions and thus fall under the illusion that the uncontrolled influx of immigrants into Western countries is for the "good" of the economy, that humans can survive on elastic wages, and that the globalisation of business and technology is positive for humanity.

They must realise that the revolutionaries of the 21st century exist—although they are not the intellectually and materially impoverished masses who the authorities seek to push down. They are members among their ranks who will revolt against their greed and destructive persistence that their power is eternal. Then, there will be hope for humankind.

This is the message that I, you, and others must send to those in the Dark Rooms. They have no choice but to consider our message. Either they must change their minds and their mindset, or they will drive everyone including themselves toward extinction from the planet Earth.

I believe that those in the Dark Rooms will come to their senses and stand by us. I believe that logic will prevail over greed and plundering. I believe that from the chaos and the ashes left, the phoenix will be reborn and we will be one step further on the path of evolution.

Chapter 3

THE HISTORIES OF REALITY

In the fields of reality, the data changes and becomes more complex. I am aware of the field of reality and at the same time, I know that your field of reality is not the same as mine at all. We live on the same planet, in the same physical space, but we have different fields of reality. Let us look at the realms of mortality in more depth.

The levels of reality

The first level of reality is animals, who perceive a completely different reality to us, one that they do not have the capacity to describe. Certainly, they do not have such concerns about the Earth or other beings as we do. They live without knowing it, with no self-awareness, no developed brain properties. They simply practice, on a daily basis, their favourite games of violence and conflict.

Though most people do not do anything differently from animals in their lives, I accept that human beings are superior to animals because of their self-awareness and other noticeable differences—the spark of consciousness and the compass of knowledge and logic.

In the case of humans, the number of fields of reality are equal to the human population. This compels us to live a socially hypocritical compromise so that we can function and communicate with each other. The average compromise is necessary to communicate with one another, but it does not mean anything more than that. It is merely our field of reality.

As noted previously, the population of our planet is over 7.54 billion humans—and that number is constantly increasing. Most people on this Earth are simple forms of intelligence because this is what the planet produces. If you want to find more sophisticated forms, you will have to either look elsewhere or create a new, more sophisticated form here, which is one of the central ideas of this book. With simple forms of intelligence, their perceptions of reality are extremely close to each other. This results in alignment, thus forming the ultimate sum of the histories of reality.

Human beings have an average level of intelligence, and they are residents in the basement of intelligence. Of course, there are "doubters" who question whether this world, this life, is all there is. Equally, there are some people with higher intelligence levels than the basement. But these humans cannot be game-changers because they compromise in their habits, social behaviours, and social morals simply to survive. Please note that when I talk about intelligence, I am not referring to the so-called "IQ" measurements. This "high IQ" hypothesis applies to losers only.

"People who boast about their I.Q. are losers."
— *Stephen Hawking*

Democratic governments

Civilisation, politics, institutions, culture, and social habits are all based on the average understanding of reality, which is the reality of people living in the basement of intelligence.

Let us take the example of democratic government as the average view of reality in a given situation. We inherited this system of democracy from the Greeks, but democracy was something completely different back then—it was the democracy of free men against women, children, and slaves. It was the democracy of wars, and not a single day passed without various kinds of conflict.

In today's democratic state, which is in deep crisis, the claimants of power (politicians) do nothing more than adapt themselves (with astonishingly adept skill) to the average value of reality. They foolishly and unashamedly mock voters by flaunting sacks of lies and promises, which they naturally know in advance they will not implement if elected. The examples are endless, and anyone can study the election speeches of candidates who won an election to see how many lies and hollow words they used to deceive voters.

Through these processes, democratic governments function. Through lies, promises, theatrics. And after the election process, through intertwining and corruption at all levels. All of this is done for a very simple reason. Politicians, elected people, presidents, prime ministers, and those "exercising power" are nothing more than puppets. They have no power for any change, only the power to obey the commands they receive from the Dark Rooms.

Of course, the elected have unique qualifications. They stand out from the crowd due to their very special "virtues", such as theatricalism, deceit, and ruffianism. They interplay between each other using the power of money, with the obvious intention of turning this interplay into complete submission. It is very easy to prove these qualities in the presidents and prime ministers of every country—just observe what they are like.

The Western democratic governments of the 21st century have fallen into processes that are void of substance or value. As the elected politicians have no real power, the only change we see after every election is a setback. We only move in reverse. Do you seriously believe that these little men and women have any power to bring about real change?

Do you look at them and laugh? Well, they are indeed ridiculous, but at the same time, do not conflate this ridiculousness with a lack of danger. They are dangerous because in the name of the supposed popular sovereignty through which they are elected, they serve their most personal and private interests in the most cruel and hideous way. They sacrifice the population on the altar of their greed, and this alter belongs to the international barons who dominate the world from the invisible Dark Rooms of world power.

In other words, world power is exercised by fire and iron every time—irrespective of who is elected as president or prime minister. Whoever that politician may be, they have the exclusive role of the puppet and the announcer of the decisions made in the Dark Rooms. Not their own decisions.

Politicians are impotent, theatrical, submissive scammers. Never forget that they come from the average reality, from the basement of intelligence. They are perfectly adapted to the average reality so that they can serve the interests of the barons of the Dark Rooms without any moral hesitation. This is why our world is in a deplorable condition with no prospect of change, only deterioration.

Yet, this democratic political system is presented to society as an achievement that must be maintained. No one dares talk about the apparent weaknesses in this political system. If you call into question this achievement, you are devoured and overthrown as a fascist. Within the framework of democratic government, it is argued that there is no reasonable alternative. In this way, control over the minds of the masses is absolute.

I know that the democratic regime has failed completely. Its current version, this kind of culture-dominated system, is a foul form of dictatorship in which the global powers of capital govern regardless of who is elected. Whoever one chooses from the mob of candidates, it is the same; there is no difference.

The electoral process has turned out to be a farce, a rallying point in which candidates are called upon to persuade the public using their theatrical talents. The people vote for the fool who convinces the public that he has the greatest talent in ridicule. Well, I do not participate in the farce that is called an "electoral process" in the context of a failed democratic system. I do not vote for any fools, nor do I position myself as a foolish candidate who is looking for figures for his "favour" in the "commons".

Controlled anarchy

The current version of democratic politics is essentially controlled anarchy. Anarchy in the area where you live, work, and vote. In this area, you are extremely vulnerable to all kinds of dangers, such as crime, violence, unemployment, and environmental damage. There are no rules here. Do not be fooled into thinking that there are rules, laws, and constitutions, as these are merely *alleged*. They are all beautiful narratives to keep you ignorant and apathetic.

Your own space, where you and your family live, is a place of controlled anarchy. In the area of controlled anarchy, you are stacked together with all of your non-privileged fellow citizens, the prey of every aspiring criminal. Keep in mind that the Dark Rooms not only feel no guilt for your circumstances, but they also come nowhere near the danger. They live far away from the area where you live, in peaceful neighbourhoods with fancy lawns and gardeners to keep them trimmed.

The system of controlled anarchy feeds on criminality and law-breaking behaviour. You, the non-privileged, do not get to enjoy social peace. You have to be constantly switched on—always keeping in your mind the possible criminal acts that may manifest against you and your family. For those in the Dark Rooms, you are merely a slave who has no right to social peace. They do not give a hoot about you.

The big cities of the Western world, where those in the Dark Rooms do not live, are places of controlled anarchy, where crowds of criminals circulate among honest and law-abiding citizens like you. While you adhere to the law with faith in the constitution and public security, criminals work upside down to denounce the law and public security.

So, instead of the system protecting you and rewarding you with honour as a law-abiding citizen, it chooses to degrade you to the criminals' plunder. You are merely a treat for the criminals who are lurking, waiting to rob you, kill you, and rape you, your wife, or your child.

If a robber invades your home and robs you at gun-point, if he commits violence against you, or he rapes you, your wife, or your child, what *rule* applies? What *law* applies? Let me tell you that *nothing* protects you. Laws and rules in a democratic regime are only punishable by other humans, and only applied after an exhaustive judicial process. They do not prevent crime and violence from happening. They have never been a true deterrent. They never prevent the aspiring killer, the aspiring robber, or the aspiring rapist.

Every criminal is free to do whatever they want—and then comes the law! Beware, the law always follows! It never comes *before*. In a democratic regime, the so-called legal order is like a carriage mounted in front of a horse.

Even if the criminal is arrested and convicted for their crimes, it is the victim who suffers during the lengthy investigative, administrative, and judicial proceedings, while the criminal enjoys the greatest pleasure in having committed the crime. Then, the laws that you believe "protect" you deliver the criminal a very mild prison sentence with a visible release horizon after which they can continue with their life! And so, for all of their diabolical acts, the criminals are "punished" with just a few years of imprisonment and are subsequently released. They are free to continue where they left off. To create new victims, new rapes, new robberies. And so the vicious circle expands.

In this way, the laws and rules do the exact opposite of protecting you. The intermittent judicial and investigative procedures, in effect, give incentives to prospective criminals by demonstrating that they may commit their crime, receive a mild punishment, then continue their life. This is the so-called "justice system".

The system of justice in the democratic system therefore pushes the criminal into their aggressive conduct against you and your family. Thus, when I walk the streets of the big cities of the Western world, I feel sorry for the honourable and law-abiding citizens because at any time, a criminal walks beside them.

The social peace of honest citizens is a deception. However, it surprises me that many citizens encounter such dangers with indifference. I am surprised by the inaction of citizens who behave as though they have asylum from criminal behaviours. They are frightened by the violent crimes that they hear about on the news every day, but paradoxically, they believe that it will not happen to them! Listen, *no one* has asylum from crime, and *everyone* is in danger at any time. If you do not understand that you are in danger, then you will likely be the next victim of criminal activity.

Well, I do not tolerate the rewarding tactics of criminals, and I will not tolerate the continuation of this horrible situation. The theories of human rights do not exist to reward criminal behaviour. Thus, when I experienced a criminal act against me, I did not merely act with indifference.

I was travelling on the London underground, when suddenly, a crazed, drunken beast with narcotic eyes began beating up the other passengers indiscriminately. When he passed by, to prevent him from attacking me, I tripped him over and pushed him to the floor. He lacked the ability to regain his posture, as his sky was apparently turning like a typhoon. So I beat him with anger and indignation. I beat him mercilessly all over his body because he was like a wild animal.

When the train stopped at the next station, I asked the other passengers—many of whom had been beaten up by this crazed beast—to help me throw him from the train carriage onto the platform. No one moved. No one responded. They were worthy of their fate. Tragically, those trifling humans were not worth my sorrow. I kicked the beast hard again and exited the train.

The beast continued his journey together with his victims. But had I continued, the police would probably have arrested me at the next station! This is the intersection of democratic processes and human rights. The authorities would have blamed me for the attack. Perhaps even locked me in their prison!

The tenants of the Dark Rooms take advantage of the fact that such beasts are circulating among us. The media, in the service of the Dark Rooms, overflow with compassion and love for the human rights of criminals. Criminals are protected by human rights despite all of their terrifying acts and heinous crimes, while you as the victim are merely a fool according to the media and some of your fellow humans. According to them, you may even be responsible for the criminal behaviour that happened to you! How many times have you heard it said of a woman who was raped that "she was asking for it"?

Understand that the democratic regime is your enemy. You are unprotected, with no immunity and no rationality in the decision of judges whose criteria is suspicious, as is demonstrated in the daily practice of the courts. If a criminal has money and connections, they never even attend court or receive a conviction. They merely pay a fine and get away with their crime. In high-profile cases, rich people are occasionally convicted to appease the public, but they are sent to "minimum security prisons" where they still enjoy many of the luxuries of their former life.

On the contrary, ordinary people from the populace are sentenced to prison terms with the greatest ease, even if the crime was not a violent one. Unsurprisingly, it is overwhelmingly the poor in society who are sentenced to prison. Men from the poorest families are 20 times more likely to be imprisoned than men from the richest families.[10]

Instead of punishing the violent criminals, judges penalise the poor bread-winners who were unfortunate enough to be involved in a messy situation, unable to pay their liabilities to the state due to poverty or a low income. Consider the billion-pound banks who file lawsuits against honourable family members who cannot afford to pay their mortgage and are forcibly thrown out of their homes for no other crime than being poor.

In critical times, the democratic system has proven to be the system of the strong against the weak in every phase of our lives. "Right" is the interest of the powerful—everywhere and always. It only applies against the weak, whether it is people, companies, or states. The powerful states decide what is "right" and impose it on the weak by force or by threat of war. You can see this happening globally, regularly, and aggressively.

Debt trading in the democratic system

You can also observe the failings of the democratic system in the issue of global debt. The world is in more debt now than ever before. There is no government that is not indebted when they are part of this international debt trading system. According to the Institute of International Finance, global debt increased by $9 trillion in 2019 to nearly $253 trillion. This includes debt from governments, companies, and households.[11]

Indeed, many households and small– and medium–sized businesses are deep in debt. That means individual people. Personally, I do not owe a cent to anyone, nor do I borrow from banks. However, my prudent attitude on the subject of self-reliance does not protect me from the fact that the government—whatever government—is indebted.

In this system, governments have delegated power to the central banks to create all forms of money. Yet these governments and banks are all the subject of private interests. The central banks are owned by the Dark Rooms. The governments are ruled by the Dark Rooms.

This is why you never hear politicians or bankers discussing the issue of being indebted or the conditions of debt trading that all the citizens of the world live in. For the puppet-politicians who act in favour of the Dark Rooms' interests, "Everything is going great!" Everything is a wonderful fairy-tale for puppet-politicians.

On account of being indebted, all governments are obliged to follow the rules of fiscal discipline. Under these rules, public spending is reduced while the cost of living and public taxes increase. As such, the standard of living for citizens is constantly in decline. In this way, the democratic political system passes government indebtedness on to its citizens, where it directly affects their wellbeing.

Yes, it is the citizens who experience the consequences of government debt, as it eventually leads to higher interest rates, lower standards of living, and higher costs for goods and services due to inflation. [12] As government debts continue to increase, now 40% higher than in 2007, things can only get worse for people in society. Yet the phenomenon of deflation in many Eurozone states is worse than high inflation, as it means that the economy in those countries is living on an oxygen ventilator.

I invite you to be alert. Do not believe that such debt is "great" for you. It undoubtedly is not.

The glacier of recession

In the previous chapter, we talked about the possible causes of the Earth's destruction, and I argued that the number one risk for human extinction is the phenomenon of expendable humanity. The second most likely reason for extinction is directly linked to the first—a general debt trading crisis that sweeps the stock markets and leaves everybody in poverty.

Governments will tell you that we can survive a recession, that we have done it before. But I will warn you that there are no capabilities to manage a new great recession like in 1929. A new recession will cause an economic freeze and an economic winter that will last for many decades. In this time of economic freeze, the human species will struggle to cope.

They will tell you that we have been flourishing and will continue to flourish. Yet, in human history, it seems that any periods of euphoria are short-lived. In the past 75 years, we created a massive bubble that has now reached explosive limits. The bubble of over-lending by governments and individuals has completed its cycle and will soon explode. We will witness a collapse of money markets, which rely on investors and funds "investing" in public debt and the future of big companies. It will collapse like a paper tower. All of the shareholders will crumble because faith in the market will crumble. Panic will dominate across the globe, creating armies of sellers at whatever price. In a matter of days, the financial model built in 1945 will collapse.

A new glacier will ravage the planet, destroying all forms of intelligent life. It will be an economic glacier. Our Earth, in just a few days, will transform from hospitable for living into inhospitable for living because of human greed and the mentality of those in the Dark Rooms, who continue to benefit from public and private debt trade.

With debt trading under their control, the Dark Rooms secure inconceivable profits. This is why I insist that the over-concentration of global wealth in the hands of a small group of people is a dangerous thing. This ever-increasing over-concentration creates a black hole for the world's unhappy citizens. Everything that circulates as money and as a productive deposit of money is absorbed instantly by the black hole of the international economic system.

Nothing can escape this black hole. Already, the black hole is at massive proportions. No information escapes outward. All money and all information about the circulation of money is trapped forever in the black hole of the financial galaxy. The only managers and controllers of the black hole are the tenants of the Dark Rooms, who have established themselves as the controllers of the circulation and seizure of money.

Because of the Dark Rooms' terrific discovery about money, they get richer day by day. They have turned money into a maze where anyone who enters is lost. They did the unthinkable. Billions of people are working to not only repay their governments' loans but also their own loans. Billions of people act as financial slaves to the Dark Rooms, effectively fuelling the black hole of our financial galaxy.

Of course, no one can predict major geopolitical changes with extreme precision, nor huge global recessions. But with the great tool of logical observation in my quiver, I see the clouds of recession thickening. The festival is over. The capacity for lending is not infinite. The capacity for central banks to continually create different forms of money is not infinite. The capacity for both governments and the private sector to repay their loans is ever more restricted.

At some point, these factors will meet. That is to say, the creation of new forms of money from central banks will cease, and the rapidly accelerating weakness of public and private debt repayment will clash violently. Together, they will cause an explosion proportionate to the collision of matter with antimatter.

I see the iceberg that is approaching, yet governments state that nothing is happening. The setting and atmosphere of their celebration and triumph of the "markets" at the expense of real, productive life is reminiscent of the luxury of the Titanic hours before it collided with an iceberg. And we will go down with it.

Why? Because you are a financial slave without even realising it. You pay your taxes so that your state can pay public debt, yet you are burdened by a decreasing standard of living. Your state is required to comply with strict financial rules, so governments reduce their spending in basic areas such as health, security, and education—the areas you rely on in life. It also reduces the system of social welfare, unemployment benefits, and pensions, which will eventually collapse.

However, make no mistake, I expect nothing from you. In the context of the social morals those in the Dark Rooms have imposed upon you, you are a happy, joyous slave. It happened to me too. A joyous slave I was! To escape your enslavement, awaken from the fake bliss you live in and start to pay attention to what is really taking place around you.

A call for revolution

For all of these reasons, I reject the democratic system, or better yet the version of the democratic system that dominates 21st century governments.

This so-called "democratic" system does not speak for, nor care for, my concerns or yours. This controlled anarchy does not work for us; the power of the strong over the weak does not work for us; the imposition of the interests of the powerful by "right", laws, and judicial decisions does not work for us; their financial systems of debt and more debt do not work for us.

We are not represented by the puppet-politicians, nor the bankers, nor the corrupt parliaments who legislate by executing orders and serving the interests of the tenants of the Dark Rooms. Mass criminality and the risk of criminals flooding into our private lives does not work for us. Global debt does not work for us. None of it works in our favour.

This is why I suggest—no, I demand—a change in the model of governance. I demand revolutionary change. I can no longer tolerate the chaotic societies that force us to live in this manner. I demand the introduction of new, strict rules where the privileged will become honourable, law-abiding citizens, where they cannot escape punishment for their criminality using the power of money.

I demand the introduction of new rules that put an end to the domination of crime. I demand that public interest must hold the stronger position, where the private interests of the powerful on Earth are in the interests of the public, the law, and justice. Not the other way around. I demand that public interest must prevail over an individual's human rights. Not the other way around.

I demand that the resources of the planet be managed prudently and reasonably so that all human beings can have access to every country in the world and if they wish, are free to remain in their beautiful home country earning a reasonable wage. Prudent and reasonable administration of resources would eliminate the over-concentration of wealth for a small group of people and global debt.

I realise that segregating personal wealth to serve the global public interest is a complicated affair. The fact is, it is a one-way road. Sooner or later, the tenants of the Dark Rooms must realise that this system of power and over-concentration is deadlocked. It will lead, with mathematical certainty, to the self-destruction of this species and the disappearance of *all* of us from the planet Earth.

Indeed, the elimination of over-concentration should be voluntary. Nothing I suggest should be done by force or coercion. These are characteristic of the outgoing politics, that is, the violence and coercion of the powerful against the weak. It would be shameless and contradictory if I proposed anything violent. I am against in any kind of violence, though as is the case of the drunken beast on the train, I reserve the right to defend myself with the maximum strength. On the contrary, those in the Dark Rooms must willingly rebalance the over-concentration of wealth.

Note that the segregation of wealth *does not* mean the total alienation of wealth. I am not proposing that we overthrow plutocratic structures. The wealthy will continue to be wealthy and can secure their own and their offspring's futures. There will continue to be wealthy maxims, but healthy maxims in an environment of balance and harmony. At the same time, these people who voluntarily handed over their excess will emerge as the new heroic revolutionary figures of history.

In this case, those in the Dark Rooms have no defence, no reasonable arguments. We must come together as a species. The tenants of the Dark Rooms must either compromise and contribute—or disappear together with us. They have neither permanent asylum nor the ability to colonise another planet. Hey folks, you cannot colonise another planet! Not now, not in a million years.

My personal goal is to pass on the peaceful alarm for our survival to enable this new history to be created. The message that we must continue to exist. Of course, I do not expect impoverished global people to contribute to the formation of the new foundations of governance or financial systems, just as I do not expect a revolution from any members of expendable humanity. By my own logic, I do not expect any contribution from those who have nothing to contribute.

The revolution of the 21st century must be against the tenants of the Dark Rooms but unlike the revolutions of the past, where the people formed an angry mob, it must be an internal revolution. It must come from the tenants of the Dark Rooms themselves! A revolution against their own mentalities will make all the difference, far more than the actions of materially destitute global people. It is time for them to stand up and be counted.

Chapter 4

THE SCOURGE OF THE MEDIA

Now you are starting to see the world for what it really is, let us look at the reality of all kinds of media, including social media and "the media". In my opinion, media is the second cataclysm after Noah's flood, the one described in the *Book of Genesis*. Noah's flood is one of the well-known myths in many religions. Yet the flood of media is real. It is not a myth. Not even close.

The age of the smartphone

In this modern era, your life is directly connected to media—social media, news apps, and the internet. You are hooked up to this media via your smartphone, which is like a hospital drip. Yes, I see you there with your smartphone in your hand. These days, it is almost impossible to operate without a smartphone in the Western world, and even in some parts of the developing world. In India, a country where two-thirds of people still live in abject poverty[13], there are over 100 million smartphone users.[14]

Over 3 billion people worldwide today own a smartphone, which is just under 40% of all the humans alive today. All of them. Consider that just 120 years ago, hardly anybody had a telephone at all, let alone a device attached to their hand for the majority of their waking hours. A decade has passed since the emergence of the smartphone and the majority of humans already report that they could not live without it, like it is a vital organ keeping them alive.[15]

I am struck by the fact that people organise their lives so that media is the foundation of their day. From morning until night, they hand over their life to various forms of media. What do people do all day on social media and their smartphones? It is one of the first things they do when they wake up. They post every facet of their life on social media. They scroll through endless "feeds" of images, adverts, and videos—"feeding" them like they *need* it. That glowing screen is the last thing they look at before they close their eyes at night. But for what?

Does any of this sound familiar, friend? Do you see how attached to your phone you are?

The average human who owns a smartphone uses it for an estimated 2.5–3.5 hours every day. This is the equivalent of a whole waking day per week. Much of this time, as you might imagine, is spent on social media. More than half of the world's global population use social media, a figure that increases with the passing of every day.[16]

This is especially true for young people, who are even more attached to their phones than adults are—as demonstrated by studies and simple observation—although the current form of social media draws people of all ages. According to research, the vast majority of young people in the Western world use social media.[17]

Yet, numerous articles and studies implore humans to put down their smartphones and pay more attention to each other and the world outside of their screen for a better quality of real life. Despite this, smartphone usage is continually increasing. Media, how many slackers have you hassled? How much of people's time have you wasted?

This is why I live without media. I reject it as a gross seizure of my time. Media sucks up your poor time before you even realise it has gone. That is not to say that you should fail to educate yourself on current world events. Importantly, you must discern the difference between educating yourself and being drawn into time-sapping exploits. For example, I read articles on the internet without accepting anything as true—merely to be aware of what others perceive as true. I follow scientific and economic developments through the media, but in the context of developing my own understanding of the world.

It is important that you understand life here in the mortal realm, and you cannot do that if you fail to pay attention to what is occurring in the world. It is time to put your smartphone down and pay attention to the world around you.

The publishing media

Within the media, there is an area of particular interest to us writers and readers—publishing. As an author, you are told that you must participate in social media to promote your book. Even the giant publishers of the world require their authors to have a public image on social media. Of course, the great writers of the past had no social media to establish a name for themselves before a publisher would offer them an opportunity. None of these great writers had the slightest media involvement, no blogs, no followers... No such thing existed.

In today's world, we are told that social media involvement is a necessity for authors. Well, I do not participate in social media because I reject it on principle. However, for the purposes of communicating with my readers, there is a website for *The Temple* that will function as a communication channel between us. My goal for this website is to help each reader cultivate their mind and evolve my teachings according to their individual genetic properties.

I am determined to make this leap to be accessible to the planet's inhabitants who feel that deep down, something is wrong. I write this book for them. They know that things are not right, but they are not strong enough or spiritually educated enough to fight against their reality. This book is their guide, and through my website, I will also assist in the emergence of new author talent, promoting truly great new writers.

Understand this, the truly great writers are not being published right now by traditional publishers. In the best case, only mediocre authors are published. The truly great writers have very unique DNA and therefore a very special, spiritual personality. As a result, they generally do not like media participation, such as social media, because they do not identify with the masses. Their own spiritual pursuits, their spiritual struggles, are in no way identical to the masses' moral and media customs. Thus, these great writers have no "platform" for their name to become known, and traditional publishers say "no thank you" to them.

As a result, bookstores—which only stock books provided by traditional publishers that they have private deals with—have become occupied by the mediocrity of our sad and decadent times. In bookshops, you will find thousands of rubbish novels and nonsense about how to get rich, get smart, and solve all of your problems without even moving off the sofa.

Why? Because publishers believe *that* is what readers want, and in many cases, they do due to their idolatrous nature. In these cases, the name of the author is what sells the book even if the book is dreadful—and even if the famous person did not write the book because a ghost-writer was hidden behind the curtain.

In some less tangible sense, readers do want to solve their problems. Deep down, many people know that something is broken and they want desperately to fix it. Only they try to fix it with money and possessions, not realising that what is broken is actually *spiritual* and no money in the world can glue it back together. (For these reasons, I did not write this book based on what readers are asking for. I decided that I would impose my position on readers regardless of the prevailing mentality because a wake-up call and a spiritual connection are what people *truly* need.)

The problem is that big publishers have very little concern for quality or truly helping humankind because publishing is about commerciality. They cannot reasonably guess which books will make them money (as demonstrated by 10 major publishers rejecting the now billion-pound franchise of *Harry Potter*), so they simply publish multitudes of books in quick succession with the hope that one of those books will be lucrative. For this reason, quality is no longer a concern—and publishers do not give their editors sufficient time to edit properly. As a result, such books contain self-contradictions and logical errors.

At the other end of the scale, self-publishing has opened the floodgates for literally any writer with an internet connection to publish a book, many of whom fail to consider the quality needed or have an editor help them uncover their ideas. You can see the effect of this in action: an overabundance of books circulating without any literary merit and by extension, commercial value.

In the modern era, the publishing world sees the unprecedented involvement of millions of people who are striving to become writers. Yes, millions of people write daily with dreams of becoming an acclaimed author. This fact is exploited by all kinds of literary merchants, who with every possible and unlikely means attempt to persuade people that whoever writes can become an author.

There are no more deceptive people in the publishing world than "vanity publishers", who prey on aspiring authors' desperation for somebody, anybody, to read their words. With this knowledge, they convince aspiring authors that they are getting a legitimate publisher, then make them part with their hard-earned money while offering little more than they would get from self-publishing.

All of this leads to the eventuality that many of the current books published lack value and distinction. Thus, when I read, I carefully choose from self-published books on online platforms—books that offer interesting content from unknown writers—and the great classical writers who are infinitely more exciting than our current counterparts.

I also read some paragraphs from traditionally published books to observe them, to see the madness of the traditional path of publishing. One of my future business plans is to create a bookstore for independent authors only. My ambition is to bring back the real, original writing talent; voices that are now forbidden and never rise to the surface due to the tyranny of traditional publishing. To regain the lost art of writing.

The lost arts

As you have seen, the general atmosphere of our times forbids the appearance or wide-scale recognition of great writers. This fact is in alignment with all other aspects of our spiritually-faltering humanity. It is also in line with the general population's inconceivable captivity in time-sucking traps such as sport, popular music, and celebrities. Our era is a time of judgment at all levels.

Personally, I am sad for my lost literary and musical loves…the legendary Abba, the Bee Gees, and the Beatles. As in literature, nothing expresses me in contemporary music. No truly great singer has the ability to make an appearance anymore for the very same reasons that affect writers. For example, a young Elvis Presley is not going to reappear any time soon. The great musicians grew up in an age where there was no internet and no social media.

Is it a coincidence that with the advent of social media, the great artists have disappeared from the foreground and their position is dominated by rubbish music? Songs in the charts are number one for months but are forgotten almost as quickly. Pop lyrics that are utterly insignificant and meaningless, and at times even derogatory. Not to mention the "auto-tune" tool used on the vast majority of pop songs, making their original singers sound manufactured, generic, and exactly the same as all the rest.[18]

It is no surprise then that University of Vienna researchers found that pop music is "becoming increasingly formulaic in terms of instrumentation under increasing sales numbers due to a tendency to popularise music styles with low variety and musicians with similar skills."[19] Another study found that since 1955, popular songs have become louder and have less variation in their structure. Of course, you only have to turn on the mainstream radio to hear this with your own ears.

Is it a coincidence that since the 1990s, great artists have been lost in all areas of the arts? The last great musician for me was Freddie Mercury. Is it a coincidence that dimwit loudmouths and noisy blokes who pretend they are great artists prevail these days? The great artists, whether they are writers, painters, or musicians, do not go with the current. They create the same current and entice other people with it. By contrast, our current era recognises and celebrates all kinds of mediocrity.

On the other hand, the few great musical artists left out there are barely heard over the noise of talent competitions, chart music, and popular culture. Like with books, music producers believe that the general public wants to listen to mind-numbing, meaningless music, so that is what they offer. Well, I am determined to go against the current. I will create the current; the current will not create me. I invite you to turn off the radio and do the same.

The demon of pornography

Unfortunately, poor-quality music and literature have become the norm in today's society. And while the loss of truly great artists is a matter of sorrow for me, it pales in comparison to the demon of pornography, another of the 21st century's accepted—and even *celebrated!*—norms.

Since the rise of the internet, the demon of pornography has become accessible at just the click of a button. Thus, in today's society, it is now considered "normal" to watch pornography.[20] In fact, one website alone called Pornhub receives 42 billion visits per year, which is a shocking 115 million per day! This is all despite many studies demonstrating that regular pornography usage can lead to mental health issues, relationship problems, lack of focus, debt, and drug abuse.

Moreover, the tragic consequences of pornography usage extend to rape, violence against women, and the hell of narcotics, which studies demonstrate are the potential effects of this new "norm". One study found that in 300 scenes from pornography films, 88% contained physical aggression against women.[21] Over the history of pornography, it has become increasingly violent, humiliating, and abusive towards women. What kind of bastards are those men who humiliate and abuse women in porn videos? And what does it say about the men who watch it?

With the ease of access to online pornography, even children are exposed to this degrading and often violent world, which in turn shapes their minds and influences their views of sexual experiences, women, and relationships. In America alone, over two-thirds of boys have watched pornography by the age of 14.[22] In this way, children are having their youthful innocence sexually exploited and forsaken.

As pornography has become normalised in society, it has seeped into other areas of daily life, such as non-pornographic movies, social media, music videos, and television. This means that children and young people are infinitely more likely to encounter this uncontrollable, cruel, and utterly disrespectful form of sexual behaviour.

With the wide-scale usage of pornography leading to violence against women and the sexual trafficking of people, we must open our eyes to the damaging consequences of pornography for all of society.

The scourge of the media

It is time to eradicate the scourge of media, social media, and pornography. These black holes contribute to spiritual apathy and even spiritual atrophy of the people of Earth. They obstruct physical choice and negate the free thought to seek higher forms of spiritual experience. Thus, I reject them outright, and I welcome you to do so as well.

If you still believe these aspects of human life to be positive or necessary, then please dedicate one day of your life to exploring them fully and with open eyes. I invite you to look for yourself at the unprecedented manipulation of public opinion in completely indifferent directions towards things that have no contribution to spiritual development. In simple terms, these things do not contribute to the significant goal of your improvement from the you of yesterday. Improving yourself compared to yesterday should be the goal of any sophisticated form of intelligence.

Engaging with the media or social media bears no relation to the sacred purpose of improvement. Instead, it systematically and programmatically pushes Earth's citizens towards becoming a mass of sheep with controlled free will. A mass of stupid idiots, tools in the service and perpetuation of the system of slavery of the 21st century.

In the case of the news media, imagine the quality of information that your mind is bombarded with daily: "news" that merely addresses the instincts of the masses and not the goal of accurately disseminating useful information. In the biggest ever study of American newspapers, researchers found that over half of all articles contained at least one mammoth error, from a lack of subjectivity in the questions asked to taking people's comments out of their original context. Similar studies have been conducted across the globe with parallel results.

Imagine the content of the daily newspapers, in both classical paper form and electronic editions. With this comparison, you can witness how they are all competitors in a meaningless game. The competition is over who has the most exciting gossip; who will deliver the most stories about rapes, crimes, and violence; who will deliver the latest news about the parasites we call "celebrities".

Worse still, such news agencies present you with increasingly negative news, and have done since the 1970s. Consider that in the days before television and social media, there was limited access to information about what was happening in the wider world. Make no mistake that crimes, rapes, and murders were occurring every day, but the masses largely had no awareness of them, thus foolish people have the perception that the world was safer in the past.

The world is no more dangerous than it was centuries ago. But we can now access the news 24/7, giving us the perception that the world is now more dangerous. Here, the question is: to know or not to know? My answer is that true knowledge of the nature of the world is vital, even when that nature is violent. However, be careful to retain your sense of perspective, and do not blindly believe everything you see and hear.

You see, the news in your individual neighbourhood or country is skewed, as the information you receive is based on which area of the world you live in. This makes such "news" extremely subjective because it fundamentally supports the politics and opinions of those living in that location. The news you receive is therefore in accordance with the interests and political direction of the owners of the media. In the UK, as an example, billionaire businessman Rupert Murdoch was the owner of major newspapers, and as an avid supporter of the Conservative government, he ensured that the news was presented in such a way that it reflected Conservative views and values.[23]

This distortion of information can also be witnessed in the media's loathing of certain countries or types of people. In America, for example, anything negative is ascribed a Russian or Chinese origin. In the case of Covid-19, President Trump famously called the virus "the Chinese virus", and his associates even named it "Kung flu".[24] This focus on the Chinese origin of the virus led to hostility against people in America who were perceived to be Chinese, including verbal insults and even being spat at in the street. Nothing more clearly demonstrates the harmful effects of the media on the gullible public's actions.

In the same manner, the UK news portrays an overwhelmingly negative image of Muslims to the public. One newspaper, *The Daily*

Mail, featured harmful or undesirable coverage of Muslim people in three-quarters of its stories.[25] Across the entire UK news industry, over half of the news was negatively inclined against Muslim people. Thus, news consumers develop the fallacious perspective that Muslims are more likely to commit crimes or violent acts against them.

It is also documented that watching negative news has a damaging effect on our minds. Those who watch the news regularly can lose their sense of perspective around crime rates, death causes, and many more important matters. The American news, for example, focuses on the destructive effects of tornadoes, and as a result, the American people hugely overestimate their likelihood of dying by hurricane (currently 50 deaths per year), while enormously underestimating far more fatal and everyday causes such as asthma (4,000 deaths per year). All sense of perspective has been lost.

Such disturbing news can also cause its viewers to become anxious, depressed, angry, and desensitized according to research by Graham Davey, a professor emeritus of psychology at Sussex University in the UK and editor-in-chief of the *Journal of Experimental Psychopathology*.[26] This professor found that today's news is "increasingly visual and shocking", with horrendous smartphone videos and audio clips of live violent events streamed to us 24/7. This pessimistic news can change our mood and even cause us to worry about events in our life that are entirely unrelated to the news. Such stress can even cause physical health problems in the delicate human body.

To avoid these harmful effects, you must try your upmost to find valuable articles. Every day, I strive to separate the useful articles from the mountains of rubbish, and of course, I find some things of value. Of course, I do not ask you to follow me in my political thesis. But I do strongly urge you to change your attitude and leave aside the hellish worlds of the media, social media, and pornography. I ask you to leave behind this extremely degraded lifestyle and find a more nourishing repast.

Only you can decide whether you are a Hollywood star who people are desperate to read about, another parasite celebrity lover, loser, and follower—or someone who charts their own path in life. Only you can choose to be discerning regarding music, literature, and art. Only you can be different from the masses who are drip-fed from their smartphones.

Hey, wake up! Who do you think you are, after all? Who do you want to be?

Consider it. Decide whatever you want. If you are ready to join the evolutionary race for intelligence, to reach higher realms and escape this violent world, proceed to Part 2.

PART 2

THE FUNDAMENTAL PRINCIPLES

Chapter 5

THE FIVE FUNDAMENTAL PRINCIPLES

No matter how many levels of education you attend and how many jobs you have, you are never taught the fundamental principles of life. These principles are a necessity to escape life on this planet. So in this part of the book, I will teach you the fundamental principles that education should be based on. These principles are applicable in the corrupt states of the 21st century and even in Plato's ideal state. They are uniformly applicable to the entire spectrum of political societies—from antiquity to today and in all possible future societies.

The fundamental principles are:

1. Communication as the supreme form of meditation.
2. Liberation from the idolatry of the present civilisation.
3. Self-reliance and a frugal lifestyle free from debt.
4. Self-awareness and self-confidence of being.
5. Continuous study of the behaviour of nature.

These principles should be the foundation of human education. The other principles of life are subject to the mind of each individual based on their physical and mental potential and the sacred means of free choice.

Fundamental Principle 1 – Communication as the supreme form of meditation

Communication with the Supreme Beings —the ultimate form of meditation—is the first fundamental principle. In this principle, you must learn to communicate with the Supreme Beings who watch over us from a place beyond understanding. To communicate with them, you must first understand that you are not some arbitrary creation of nature. If you visualise yourself as being so low—just a random, vile speck in the universe—then the fundamental principles will fail to work, and you will cease to be part of the cosmic plans. Of your own free will, you will fall under the category of "vile speck in the universe".

You must also understand who and what these Supreme Beings are, and where they reside. They live in the **conscious realm**, which is half of the pair of our material universe. There are mortal realms everywhere in the material universe. They are planets similar to our Earth, and they are friendly to the development of life and intelligent life. In these mortal realms, consciousness is a colonist.

By contrast, the conscious realms are planets everywhere in the evolved universe. They consist of evolved matter, evolved particles, evolved natural laws, evolved logic, and evolved intelligence. They are hospitable for the development of conscious life, and they are the original homeland of consciousness. Consciousness is the master.

The Supreme Beings are all of an equal intelligence level but have different duties. This is an evolved level from what we hold in the mortal realms. They have specific duties to follow in observing all of the mortal realms, such as conducting experiments on us, supporting those who ask for help, and coming to the mortal realms as colonists in the brains of those with the capacity to host them (which you will learn more about later). They have the ability to travel in time anywhere, everywhere, in the past and present of all mortal realms.

The Supreme Beings have a governing body called the Society of the Composers, who live in the Temple of Consciousness. These Composers deal with advanced duties, such as designing and controlling all kinds of material universes and conscious realms. The Society of Composers never deals with inhabitants of the mortal realms.

[78]

Thus, we can understand that the dualities are:

material universe — evolved universe

mortal realms — conscious realms

anthropic laws — non-anthropic laws

intelligence — evolved intelligence

known, observable — unknown, not observable

The inhabitants of the mortal realms must progress and expand their level of consciousness and intelligence to reach the conscious realms. As their compass, they have **logic**, which is the greatest gift of consciousness. This compass can help us to traverse the tempestuous oceans we face in life and reach our goals. Our ultimate goal is to move forward—expanding our intelligence and consciousness, evolving forever until we qualify for the conscious realms.

For the vast majority of people, this target is not realistic unless they spend the lifetime length of two or three universes training in other mortal realms. This measurement is neither quantifiable nor accurate; it simply means that your evolutionary journey is not a matter to be hunted. Hunting time is always impossible, and it is a trap that common people untrained in spiritual experiences get snared by.

The point is that it is never too late to start the journey of evolution. When you start, you never move backwards, only forwards. This means that your next journey in a mortal realm will be undertaken in better conditions than your current ones—and so on until you reach the conscious realms. You see, the Supreme Beings were once like us; they lived in the mortal realms and eventually qualified to live in the conscious realms. The residents of the conscious realms were once like you, and your privilege is that you can become like them if you follow the evolutionary way.

Of course, some people choose not to evolve—either through ignorance and a lack of education or due to the arrogant mentality of our current science that almost everything is solved and that nothing exists after our departure. These people will be forced to move backwards in the worst conditions to start over and over again in the mortal realms unless they decide to evolve. Note that this does not relate to karma. You do not need to be a criminal to move backwards. Whether criminal or innocent victim, if you do not evolve, you will move backwards to start the evolution trial again.

The process of communication

To evolve, you must learn to communicate with the Supreme Beings. Usually, communication with Supreme Beings is referred to as prayer or meditation. You may refer to it in any way you choose. The important thing is that communication is a form of spiritual exercise, and so it requires *persistent efforts* to deliver results. Your spiritual exercise should be continuous and not suffer interruption. It must be carried out on a daily basis, so it is your prerogative to set aside time every day or night for this spiritual exercise.

In the early stages of your practice, you will not get tangible results, but you must continue with optimism and strength nonetheless. If you continue, you will receive the results—messages from on high—but this will not happen immediately. Remember, the Supreme Beings do not live on Earth, and you do not have an antenna to receive their messages. These things take time.

Assuming that you conduct your spiritual exercise consistently, at some point you will perceive that you are constantly in communication with a Supreme Being throughout the day. However, this lasting communication should not be your goal at the beginning. Instead, it will calmly manifest on its own and spontaneously emerge, like a new type of energy reserve.

The messages, when they arrive, are like packages filled with powerful knowledge. You will receive these packages in your mental mail via the higher channels, which some religions call "the Holy Spirit". The contents of these packages will initially surprise you in the powerful knowledge they contain. In many cases, this knowledge will be different from your expectations. You will expect one thing, but something completely different will arrive because of the huge distance that separates your understanding from their advanced level of intelligence.

Please do not be dismayed if the messages do not match your expectations. As a more advanced form of intelligence than you, the Supreme Beings send messages appropriate for your inherent capacity for absorption. They possess and manage the information, and they exist in stark contrast to you, who lacks innumerable pieces of information at any given moment.

Intelligent humility

Although the Supreme Beings are far more advanced than you, they have chosen you from the plethora of other forms of intelligence (animals, trees, birds, fish, matter) to discover them. If you discover them and ask for their help, you are destined for success, so please acknowledge this and be humble, something that many humans struggle to achieve.

Yes, human beings have discovered natural laws. Bravo, well done! However, this does not mean that the Supreme Beings will tolerate any manifestation of arrogance from humans. Although humans have discovered the natural laws that apply uniformly throughout the universe (with the exception of gravity, as the nature of it is an unsolved mystery according to my observations), the great paradox is that they ignore their own polluted, dirty, and horrid nature, which is essentially no different from that of an animal, no matter how it is dressed up.

The hypocrisy is unbelievable; humans are so pitiful and so ridiculous. They get sick from the slightest cause and are vulnerable to all kinds of accidents. They leave their house in the morning—getting rid of their horrid stench in the bathroom first—with absolutely no guarantee of returning home unharmed. Thus, you should never overestimate what a common, vulnerable animal the human being is.

Instead, we must always be conscious of where we stand and vigilant of what is happening around us in this mortal realm. Look around you. How much do you value the human beings you see? Note that you are not being asked to have complete scorn for your fellow humans. Total scorn for this realm does not suit you. Yet, at the same time, you need not see value where there is none. You have to be humble and kind to evolve, but not stupid. Thus, I propose a new approach of *intelligent humility*.

Your spiritual exercise should not be isolated or removed from the mortal realm. We must never ignore or give away the needs and fights of our everyday lives relating to people and circumstances. We must never behave as monks isolated from the modern world. We are at the same time inside and outside of the modern world. We are not designed to be cut off from the mortal realm, nor should we relinquish it to dark forces.

At a highly developed level of communication, the practitioner will simultaneously experience both the spiritual and the mundane, and they will have the reassuring awareness of the power of the higher laws and their supremacy over human knowledge.

The laws of communication

As the Supreme Beings do not reside on Earth, they are not bound by the natural laws that apply on Earth or in our universe. Of course, they are bound by laws, but not ones known to you. Higher laws override lower ones, and higher intelligence imposes laws on lower intelligence. We, the inhabitants of the mortal realm, should not, and cannot, question the laws governing the Supreme Beings.

Likewise, the laws governing the arrival of packages of knowledge are not subject to examination or investigation, nor is any expression of interest in us by a Supreme Being. Every effort toward its examination will end up in a foolish and unhelpful state of despair. The arrival of such packages is governed by higher laws that are unknown to humans.

All you need to understand is that these laws are the reason why the Supreme Beings will not grant everything you ask for. They will not send you a shipload of gold, nor will they give you the lucky numbers for the lottery. These are the foolish desires of idolaters.

Accepting the existence of the higher laws, I receive the packages not as a result of research and investigation, but as a spontaneous verification in my brain. It absorbs the packages that arrive as a pleasant surprise, taking no interest in the route they took before their appearance in the appropriate place. Spontaneous verification occurs in every genuine exercise of communication with the Supreme Beings.

Through this communication with Supreme Beings, your level of perception will expand to an unbelievable degree, and your consciousness will expand everywhere and forever. Moreover, you will always experience spontaneous protection beside you. You will not be alone here on Earth. You will have a protector who acts on your behalf and directs you to the right choice, which often would not otherwise have occurred to you.

The beautiful thing is that these advanced forms of intelligence concern themselves with you even though you are lower than them. In fact, they are so advanced that they simultaneously communicate with and provide protection to plenty of other humans as well as you. This is possible under their laws.

The law of logic dictates that a higher form such as a Supreme Being cannot descend to the level of a lower one because they are evolved, neutral beings. Yet, logic does not prohibit engagement between higher and lower forms when those on high agree to it. We are free to seek out these beings and request their guidance and blessings, and they may respond generously and richly with spiritual treasures. We cannot judge them as it is not within our scope. Nor can we guide or bless a Supreme Being, as such guidance is only applicable in one direction.

Understand that your job in all of this is to evolve. However, this does not mean the biological evolution of your species—but the lasting, intellectual, spiritual development of you as an individual. I believe this is part of natural law and that the spontaneous emergence of new physical properties is the result of communicating with Supreme Beings. Thus we, the educated mystics of spiritual experiences, can constantly experience the spontaneous appearance of powers throughout our lives.

To maximise your brain's potential to turn our spark of consciousness into a fire, you should practice mental exercise and training on a continuous basis. There are no restrictions on the conscious realms, and our quest for consciousness can extend to the eternal depths of the higher worlds. So, start practicing now.

Fundamental Principle 2 – Liberation from the idolatry of the present civilisation

Of course, to devote sufficient time to your mental exercise and practice, you must stop wasting time on idolatry.

Your life mortal life is completely idolatrous. Have you ever pondered over that? Do you realise that the authorities are pushing you very skilfully and very forcefully toward the deification of idols? These are the idols that you believe in passionately: money, glory, fame, sex, glamour, luxury, gluttony, music, football, social media, your career, and many other things that are applauded by the mainstream. And you unknowingly invest everything in their worship.

Your entire life revolves around idols, whether you realise it or not. Your goals are to be part of this idolatrous mentality. Your family is also part of this idolatry, as is your school, college, workplace, and social circles. As you saw earlier, education is crucial, but it is used by the masters in the Dark Rooms to shape you into an idolater—so corrupt and far from natural freedom that there is not a single second left to breathe or think for yourself.

For the sake of integrating you into spiritually maimed idolatry from your infant years, even your family is "offered up". Education works exclusively on stock market terms. It forces you to invest all of your energy, your resources, and the freshness of your youth in one share: the share of idolatry. Either you invest all of your energy in this share or you better watch out, because the authorities do not permit non-conformity.

To keep you feeling special, the authorities ensure that you are important on specific dates. Think of your childhood birthdays, Christmases, and all the holidays that the system imposes on you. On these special days, people give you gifts, take countless photographs, sing to you, and make you feel important. I am sorry to inform you that in reality, you are no more than a consumable resource.

Unfortunately, the authorities in the Dark Rooms have malevolent and fraudulent intentions for your family, which is their favourite institution. They know the strength of the long-term bonds between parents and their children, even stronger than that between spouses.

No parent in the world is not interested in the well being and happiness of their children (so long as they are logical people who adhere to social standards, of course). In this way, nature has ensured that the bond between you and your children is as strong as a nuclear force. You would do anything to ensure that they never lack basic necessities.

Since ancient times, religions have supported the institution of the family to increase the number of believers under their authority. Similarly, those in the Dark Rooms know all too well that your family is your Achilles' heel. They want you to be busy 24 hours a day—and contributing to the well being of your family means investing more time. In the morning, you go to work, and in the evening, you are occupied with your children. There is little personal time left over for you. The authorities then offer you "rest" from the fatigue of the day and your commitment to your children and spouse through the television and the smartphone.

Television—in both the traditional edition of limited channels, the older edition of a cable subscription, and the newer edition of an internet connection—is the primary means of your entertainment. Through it, you are persuaded to worship garbage that is presented to you. What is more, you even offer your children entertainment that has been deemed a necessity by the system. Even the news is presented to make you think for or against issues according to the channel owners' interests. This is why I never watch the trash on TV.

Likewise, I choose to be "informed" by reading the news online, but I never take it at face value. Instead, I use the news to find out what other people believe to be facts. Simultaneously, this knowledge arms me to repudiate whatever is presented as "real" in the everyday madness of this planet. I therefore choose to create facts, not accept what others have created for me. I invite you to do the same, rather than accepting as facts things that are nothing more than fiction.

Understand that those in the Dark Rooms want to ensure that your weekdays are packed, and they take care of your weekends too! Ideally, you should not be free even for a second. This is why they ensure that sports stars take over your time and your mind. Today's sports stars are no different from the gladiators of Ancient Rome. Football players and the like are the gladiators of the modern era.

If you look closely, the worship of football is happening in dedicated temples in every city and village across the world—they are called stadiums. Every city and village of the world may not have a hospital, but you can bet there is a football field! The authorities have initiated you in the worship of football so you cannot live without it. The intensity of worship can vary from person to person, but it is prevalent at an almost global level.

(Note that this also applies to other activities such as gambling and other sports such as basketball. In fact, gambling has infested the domain of sports like a catastrophic blight—so much so that it operates hand in hand with *every* sport. Gambling does not say no to anyone and has many victims. It is bizarre how many people believe that they will be victorious over probabilities in the long term.)

So, the worship of sports, particularly football, is a universal phenomenon. You ask yourself "How much do these stars deserve to be paid?" You feel exasperated upon hearing how much they were signed for, yet you still watch them! Your defence may be "I don't go to the stadium. I just watch the game on TV with my friends and family." But whether you watch it from your house or the bar, there is no difference. Since the goal of those in the Dark Rooms is to steal your time, the key point is that you watch it. Besides, the TV may at some point completely replace physically spectating at stadiums. Even this has been accounted for, which is why Homeric fights between media titans take place over who secures the TV rights of so-called "main events".

I do not watch football, just as I would not have watched the gladiators of Ancient Rome. The duels were strategized to steal the citizens' time so the idea of insurrection—revolution against the corrupt regime—did not cross their minds.

While the gladiators enjoyed special privileges such as companionship with women and gourmet food, they also had to undergo harsh training. The likelihood of being killed in the next match was no concern to them, and they had no anxiety about death. Even modern football players have this mindset. They run into the stadium with little concern for the possibility of getting injured, perhaps seriously. What kind of person enters an arena knowing in advance that they may be seriously injured? Have you ever wondered this or asked those around you?

Thus, I reject football idols, and I encourage you to reject them and stop wasting your own time. I am not asking you to be an ascetic here; you are not wise enough to attain nirvana. But I do ask you to consider how these idols are used just as the gladiators were used. They are used fraudulently by those in the Dark Rooms so that you have no time to think about a revolution or rebellion against them.

Of course, this does not mean you must stop watching sports in its entirety. Some sports in moderation are fine—everything is good in its proper amount. Personally, I enjoy watching tennis in moderation, selecting tournaments and watching the battles between the top players. It is an individual sport that highlights technique, strength, and spiritual virtues. However, I always watch tennis games calmly without considering any athlete either as a hero or an idol.

The athlete I like the most is Federer, and I enjoy every moment of his games. He is a genius at tennis, and I believe that no one else will appear like him in the future. There is no one else who has such rare qualities in the sport of tennis. But if I saw a tennis player anywhere except on the court, for example, when I saw Federer by chance at an international airport, I look elsewhere. I am not interested in their private lives, their opinions, or anything but their matches.

The key is to not give up all (or much) of your free time on these distractions. And importantly, steer clear of the worship of idols, be it in football, basketball, or any other arena. Review your attitude regarding pseudo-idols, reject them with all of your heart, and shout with a voice of thunder "Never again!" Rest assured that no pseudo-idols made by mortals have the slightest value. They are just colossal illusions.

Likewise, why do you believe that whoever can sing, has a talent for insincerity, and appears on the silver screen is more important than you? Why do you stand and applaud like a fool? Why do you read the tabloids and ramblings of "professional" writers because they are bestsellers? The best writers in the world have never been published, as you have learned.

The real talents live and walk among you. You see, I like music, but I am selective about what I listen to. I like the theatre, but I am equally selective about what I watch. At the same time, I never consider myself inferior to anyone. But not because I have a big ego. On the contrary, disbanding the notion of the ego is one of the pillars of my teachings, as you will see in chapter 8.

I read books and articles on the web, but nothing that "promises" what has not been accomplished by the person making the promise. I do not buy bestsellers or the works of those who state they will transform me into a rich genius. I am infinitely richer and more intelligent than them because I am constantly training myself to reject them and their attempts to deceive me.

Ultimately, the pervasive idolatry of our era is detrimental to your evolution and to your communication with the higher powers. Throw such idolatry into Tartarus and do not look back. Reject all of the idols that those in the Dark Rooms offer you.

Fundamental Principle 3 – Self-reliance and a frugal lifestyle free from debt

As you saw in the previous chapter, the Dark Rooms seek to control your life and absorb your time through every means possible. One of their main methods of control is financial. The need for money—for basic survival and the luxuries the system says you *need*—is what keeps you working for most of your weekdays. It is what takes up the majority of your waking hours. This means that if you become financially free and self-sufficient, you can break the shackles of the system. You no longer rely on the system. You no longer need to take part.

In order to be self-sufficient and financially self-reliant, you must have the complete package of basic education. For those who are currently uneducated in spiritual experiences and financial matters, the phrase "it's never too late" is applicable—it is never too late to learn and apply the fundamental principles in your life.

The basic package of education regarding finances is knowledge of all the economic theories and models that apply in the mortal realm.

You can gain this knowledge by reading books, blogs, and articles from specialists, and also by following everyday events in the global economic area. However, you should not accept any theory to be true at face value. It is only through personal observation that you should determine a theory to be true or false.

Thus, when you have some basic training under your belt, you can begin observing the economic behaviours first-hand and teaching yourself using the bottom-up method. This method can be used to search for the answers to all questions. This way, you can access infinite self-learning. The bottom-up method gives you the opportunity to learn by seeking answers through the Spontaneous Forces. By contrast, scientists and mathematicians blindly follow conventional models and accept them as accurate. This limited view means they miss gigantic opportunities to uncover knowledge. An unlimited potential for learning will put you light years ahead of such scientists and mathematicians.

As you will see in your new learning method, the economic environment of the 21st century is extremely brutal. As talented, innovative, and fortunate as any daring investor in a new venture may be, it is extremely difficult—almost infeasible—to succeed in the long run. This is why only 4% of businesses make a million pounds and only 25% survive over 15 years[32], even in a "financially stable" country such as the UK[33]. The financial zone is economically congested as those in the Dark Rooms have extended their economic dominance into every corner and inch of the planet.

You will quickly see from monitoring the world's economic environment that you have no margin for error. Wealth outside of the Dark Rooms is rare. They have left the minimum possible amount for circulation, so your share—like everyone else's—is small and volatile. If you make a mistake, you lose your share.

In the beginning, it is critical to arm yourself against those in the Dark Rooms. You cannot allow them to capture you. But have no fear; they do not know you personally, so they will not set a trap for you. To them, you are just another fool among the 7.5 billion fools in the world. They are not interested in what the fools do in their private and personal lives; they simply set the rules of the game for themselves to win.

In order to evade capture in the long term, you must embed self-sufficiency in your DNA. Self-sufficiency and financial self-reliance can be achieved by living a simple and natural life without fanfare, exhibitions, and splurges on the non-existent needs imposed on you by the idolatrous system. Self-sufficiency is governing your financial steps with logic and prudence.

Self-sufficiency and financial self-reliance mean that you must *always* consume less than what you produce. If you exhaust your entire output, then you are not self-sufficient. The cornerstone of this principle is to always have a strategic stock of resources that you can use in emergencies. You must always have plenty reserved as savings, like a strategic stock of life.

The avoidance of banks and debts

For most humans, finances mean banks. But understand this: the banks are the property of the Dark Rooms. There is no bank that is not controlled and directed by the Dark Rooms. In order to have complete control, they set up central banks in every country, federation, and monetary union, such as the Eurozone.

Through the central banks, those in the Dark Rooms control both the circulation and the attributes of money. Money has many properties: it can be cheap, expensive, accessible, or inaccessible. All of these properties are decided in the Dark Rooms through their puppets, the central bank boards. If you research the shareholders of such banks, you will only find the apparent shareholders, not the ones behind the scenes, the people who truly rule the banks of the Western world. This small group of people control the money, its movement, and its properties, and they are shareholders in all the behemoth companies of this world.

As you will learn when studying economic models, self-sufficiency cannot be achieved when you borrow from a bank. Remember that those in the Dark Rooms constantly create fake needs through idolatry, and such needs force you to get bank loans and credit cards. Make no mistake, if you take a bank loan, you are chained to that bank. It is the same as owing money to Satan.

Banking behaviour has always been underhanded and predatory. The debtor is the prey in the mouth of a terrible predator. I understand this because I have experienced captivity to a bank. I made the mistake of borrowing money and that long period of debt was the most difficult period of my life. When I accepted a loan from that bank, I looked Satan in the eyes.

Before taking out a loan, think about how much energy you will spend dealing with and paying it back. Think of the murderous stress this process will cause, which may be prolonged for many years. Think about the negative consequences it could have on your health and your personal integrity. Think about the cost of borrowing, the size of the burden it will place on your income, and the inevitable decline in your's and your family's standards of living.

Multiple studies have found that debt has a hugely negative effect on physical health and mental health, from anxiety to blood pressure to lowering your immunity to health conditions.[27] My own modelling suggests that debt is the greatest risk factor for cardiovascular diseases and cancer due to stress flooding the debtor's system and damaging the body's bio-electric systems.

Of course, this risk also extends to mortgages for houses, which are essentially long-term loans to "own" your home. A mortgage means you are chained to the bank for the duration of the loan, which can be painful, stressful, and bad for your health and energy. Moreover, there is no guarantee that everyone will have a stable income to pay the mortgage over two or three decades.

By contrast, renting a house may mean that by the end of the month, you are free. It may also mean you are chained to your landlord, paying the same or more than you would to the bank. For the fortunate, they own their house through inheritance, but this is not realistic for the majority of people. The key point here is to understand what you are signing up for and choose the lesser of the two evils, since your mortal body must have somewhere to reside. Choose the option that results in the least debt, preferably no debt, and that will cause the least stress, preferably no stress.

The Eurozone disaster

In the Eurozone, the banking situation is particularly disastrous. In 2013, new conditions were introduced by the Euro group stating that a depositor of over 100k euros would become an investor of the bank at the same time. This inevitably means they carry the danger (the same danger as all investors) of losing their money if the bank collapses.[28]

Thus, in the Satanic context of banking, the depositor has a new identity—the investor! They invest not just in themselves, but in the prospects and risks of the bank where they have placed their savings. This may give them hardships and burdens to last an entire lifetime. Moreover, you automatically become an investor in the prospects and risks, not only of the bank but the whole Eurosystem.

Originally, politicians invested in the idea of a united Europe by creating a monetary union called the "Eurozone", but their creation quickly became a monster. The idea of European principles and values overwhelmed the harsh reality that a monetary union of independent states with very different economic structures is not viable. Creating a common currency between countries that have nothing in common is a guarantee that the Euro is doomed to die sooner rather than later, and it will cause an enormous disaster for the member states and their citizens.

My models (especially the unconnected boxes model, which you will learn about in Fundamental Principle 5) predict that the Eurosystem will collapse soon, and that any loans will be sold to other banks. Citizens' deposits will vanish and be seized by debtors who have borrowed huge sums. The collapse of the Eurosystem will cause chaos, and the banks will do whatever they can to save whatever they can.

Accordingly, only madmen and the suicidal would invest in or borrow from a Eurosystem bank. When you place your savings in any Eurosystem bank, you automatically bear the risks that plague the banking institution you have chosen in your naivety. If the Eurozone vanishes into thin air, then your deposits will disappear, and it will be impossible to take them to court and claim for damages.

Of course, it is almost impossible in Europe to be paid your wages outside of a banking institution. In fact, it is almost impossible not to use the services of banks. As such, you will most likely have to use them, but use them carefully, never trust them, and never love them.

Go forth with prudent steps! Self-sufficiency and financial self-reliance are certainly not achieved through bank loans and debts. Use all of your power to have a healthy private life, practice the profession that suits you, and always respect nature and your fellow humans, for you are not yet so sophisticated as to devalue everything. It is time to understand the true value in things.

The law of charity

You understand by now that fame, money, and material possessions do not appear when you hunt them, and that they arise in the course of events that follow from attracting the Spontaneous Forces into your life. You also know by now that the desire to pursue such material goods is a destructive mentality that has been imposed on you by the system, which is transforming you into an idolater without you even realising it. Besides, even if these idolatrous goods are accrued, they have no value beyond illusion. That is why when they spontaneously arise to mystics, they are managed differently—through charity.

However, charity is not without criteria. Charity does not work as give, give, give; take, take, take. This is not charity; it is foolish behaviour that ultimately helps neither the giver nor the receiver. Make no mistake, charity comes with specific rules. The receiver of the charity must demonstrate humble and appreciative behaviour towards the giver. They must change the way they see the world and transform their behaviour. These are the rules for accepting charity. Then, the giver will feel satisfied when they see the joyful eyes of those who genuinely benefit from their charity.

Not a day has passed in my life when I have not done at least one small charitable deed. For beginners, it is important to understand that charity has many forms beyond providing financial assistance to those in need. Charity can manifest itself in thousands of ways as human needs are incredibly diverse. You can provide aid according to your means, which could be expressing your love in whatever way you can or by getting out and providing assistance in your community. Do what you can to spread hope—give a smile, offer warmth and peace, and become the light of the world.

Spend your time spreading hope and love to your fellow humans and offering charity in your own way, rather than watching idols on TV or on the field. Practice your communication with the supreme beings and offer your time to charity, rather than to idol worship. This is the evolutionary way.

Fundamental Principle 4 – Self-awareness and self-confidence of being

To achieve success in life, you need to build the mechanisms of self-awareness and self-confidence, which are the forgotten virtues of the Ancient Egyptian Pharaohs and their engineers. You have to go back to Ancient Egypt as a young Moses to tear the sea in two, and create a path in the middle. In one part of the sea, throw the anthropic principles and Western science. In the other part, throw away the current version of the democratic system and the failed versions of Western civilisation.

Once you do this, you will be a legend like Hermes Trismegistus. In front of you will be the path—with an unlimited view and a white horizon. Nothing will appear as an obstacle before you as long as you have thrown such obstacles into the sea forever. No religion, no ideology, no regime of coercion of tyranny will interfere with your path to triumph. No annulment of the natural freedom of your mind. Here, you will experience the natural freedom of exploration of beings and matter to reach the evolution of intelligence and consciousness.

The mechanism of self-awareness

To reach this level, you need to activate and commit to the mechanism of self-awareness. With the passing of the years and constant spiritual pursuits and experiences, a person may be transformed into a mystic of spiritual powers. However, the acquirement of self-awareness cannot be determined by the Earth's measurement of time. Self-awareness is not acquired overnight. It emerges as powerful knowledge over time.

When you have acquired true self-awareness, you recognise both nature and your own nature. You have a powerful knowledge of *who I am, what I am doing here, and where I am going.* This puts you in a better position among the crowd. You know what your position is and the position of others.

You are aware of all of the chemical properties of your brain, and therefore of all the talents, weaknesses, and potential ailments that endanger your body. You take preventive measures to shield your earthly body from invasive diseases and abnormalities. You become the elected controller of your body and nullify the randomness that rules the lives of the spiritually uneducated and untrained.

You also experience the quality of the species that you belong to. With terror, you discover that the Homo sapiens species is very low on the cosmic scale of intelligence and consciousness. This makes you disillusioned, but at the same time, you recognise and understand who the other, ordinary people are. The bad news is that you belong to the lowest level in the cosmic scale. The good news is that other species are at an even lower level, as they are not even aware of how low they are.

Thus, you know for certain—from the level of self-awareness feasible here in the mortal realms—that you are an evolutionary point above animals on Earth. This also explains the intimacy between animals and humans. They are so close on the scale of evolution. Animals and humans are only a step apart! Just look at our beloved pets. Yet at some point, human animals evolved because they were judged capable of carrying the burden of consciousness. With self-awareness, you truly understand this burden.

The mechanism of self-confidence

To develop spontaneous self-confidence, you must practice and apply the five fundamental principles in your everyday life. But firstly, you have to finish reading this book! There is no other way. Read this book and follow the commandments carefully.

I will give you the very precious axiom I apply in my private life: "careful vs. casual". Who else has spoken to you before like I am talking to you now through the various and shocking concepts of this book? Nobody, and no one will after me, but do not worry about that at all. I will publish many other books. I will be your stable friend, supporter, and advisor-coach for the spiritual wars so that you may be the winner. However, please allow me to remain invisible to you, and respect my nature as an Aspergian (which you will learn about soon).

Although I am your spiritual advisor-coach, self-confidence means that if you think you have something very important to share—an idea, a suggestion, or even advice—then please email me. All I ask is that you are kind, smart, and humble in your message, otherwise I will not reply.

With spontaneous self-confidence and kindness, you can find the people who will help you on your journey of evolution. You simply have to ask for help from the Spontaneous Forces and use your self-confidence to make the right choice.

There are many applications of spontaneous self-confidence in life, but we will explore two here as examples. In the first case, your self-confidence shows you when it is best to trust your own skills and knowledge. In the second case, it shows you when to seek help and gives you the means to find that help.

The first case: The barber

I shave my face every day, as do many men. This means I know every detail, every angle, every peculiarity of my face. I can achieve a perfect, deep, and tender shave—most of the time with my eyes closed. With only the touch of a hand, I place the razor at the appropriate point on my face. During the shave, I think about the various issues that will concern me during my day or I listen to the news, with its daily stories of madness on this planet. After shaving, I apply moisturiser and let my skin absorb it for 10 minutes.

However, one time, I decided to try my neighbourhood barbershop. The barber was an experienced man around the age of 70. Certainly, he had shaved thousands of faces in his life. Yet, when the shave began, he quickly made the first mistake, then the second, then the third. With some swipes of his razor, I felt pain and fear! I kindly asked him for the punishment to end, and thankfully, I escaped the barbershop with only a few scratches and cuts.

My logical conclusion, through self-confidence, was that I know all of the details, angles, and behaviours of my face, and I am the best barber in the world—but only for my own face! Not for anybody else's face! By contrast, the barber has a general perception, the average perception of shaving based on a total of the many thousands of customers' faces he has shaved. Trust your self-confidence and do not let someone else take the razor. You know your face best.

The second case: The editor

Trying to find an editor who fits the character of this unique book was a titanic, lengthy effort. Disappointments followed one after another. With thousands of choices, I felt momentarily lost, and I was almost ready to leave the choice to chance—or even to abandon writing the book altogether. Yes, this crossed my mind.

On a daily basis, and many times during the day, I wondered how I would choose the editor who would be my spiritual match from the crowd. I tried everything—reading information and testimonials, asking for samples. The results were disappointing every time. Not only did they not satisfy my requirements in the samples, but usually they irritated me too. Most could not comprehend elementary parts of the book's personality. Some made outrageous comments underestimating my intelligence. Some thought they were the author and I was just a random passer-by on the way!

Yet, I refused to give up. I locked myself in a room to meditate and communicate with the Supreme Beings, and I called on the Spontaneous Forces to help me find the right editor. Spontaneously, a light was born! After several weeks, the light became bright in one editor. She was pointed out to me by the Spontaneous Forces. I immediately realised this was who I was looking for with so much anxiety and so much passion.

The search had come to an end. I did not need a sample. She was it. Strengthened by spontaneous self-confidence, I immediately made a deal with her. Through the few emails we exchanged, my confidence in the choice increased. (Anyone who wants to can contact her to get this confirmation for themselves on the Composers page at the end of the book.)

The case of the two black flamingos

Your self-awareness and spontaneous self-confidence extend to matters of your physical body and your mind. Look friend, it is very important to know your body's behaviour. To achieve this, you need self-awareness of how your body works and the self-confidence to be wary of people who try to take advantage of you, especially if their aim is to empty your pockets of cash.

In these cases, you will be very lucky if they only take your money. They could destroy you completely. Whether it is someone fraudulent or simply clueless, the damage done to you is the same. So, if you are diagnosed with an illness by a doctor, always do your own research.

I will share my personal story to illustrate this further. I have the rare combination of bipolar disorder and Asperger's syndrome, which is beyond the edge of what a human being can afford or handle. Here, I give you my estimation of these disorders based on my personal experience. Note that I am *not* giving advice to anyone on how to cure bipolar disorder or Asperger's syndrome. I am not authorised to give you any advice. I can only tell you about myself and my experience, and my point is that only *you* can fully understand your experience.

Science says that Asperger's syndrome belongs to the autistic spectrum, but this is not a complete explanation. Asperger's is a spectrum itself. But again this is not complete. Every individual with Asperger's is a spectrum in themselves! They are a planet in themselves, and while they have relationships with the other planets, they usually have some separate, unique qualities not found in any other Aspergian.

While scientists and psychologists have their own classifications, in my opinion, there are two main phases in the Asperger's spectrum: the mild and the wild (or the "full-blown" as some prefer to call it). Both mild and wild are again spectrums in themselves! The majority of people with Asperger's are in the mild phase. A minority of Aspergians are in the wild phase, and they may have severe social and mental difficulties.

In my early life, for decades in fact, I went without medication for either disorder. As a result, they were at their most aggressive, wild level. They were full-blown black circles, two black flamingos in the pool of my genes. While there is no official medicine for Asperger's syndrome, I later found out by understanding my body that the antidepressant medication Citalopram works perfectly and moderates the wild phase, making it mild in terms of social interactions.

At the mild level, where the vast majority of Aspergians are, a few are boosted by other genetic factors and qualities. This results in them being geniuses, especially in the area of information technology—such as Bill Gates and Mark Zuckerberg. These people are world-changers.

At the wild level, there are also those who are boosted by other genetic factors and qualities. They go in the exact opposite direction to most wild Aspergians and end up as geniuses who change the world, such as Albert Einstein and Paul Dirac. However, the Einsteins among us are very rare. Many psychologists believe that Einstein had Asperger's.[29] If you doubt that Einstein was Aspergian, listen to his talk in America in 1942 on YouTube. You can hear his unique Asperger's voice, with the specific voice tone that is the same as me and my father, and many other males Aspergians as well.

In women, Asperger's is generally mild. My cousin Katrina has Asperger's as well. She lives successfully and enjoys a normal social life. For me, the syndrome pushed me to the stage of feeling like an anti-human. However, note that women with Asperger's can also start to behave differently, shift towards self-isolation, or feel like an anti-human.

As you can see between me and Katrina, Asperger's is a spectrum. In fact, many syndromes and disorders are spectrums. Did you know that diabetes type 2 is a spectrum as well, although most diabetes doctors fail to disclose this fact to their patients? This is why I state that every patient must get personal treatment for each syndrome and disorder. There should no longer be general treatment.

Likewise, bipolar disorder is a spectrum—one that I inherited from my mother. She is a simple woman with a good, pure, original Cypriot Turquoise heart. She is full of love for everybody, and she is very healthy and active at the age of 86 under Citalopram.

I once wrote that a human being in the depression phase of bipolar is the most miserable species in the whole universe. Thankfully, I have almost eradicate my episodes of mania or depression due to this medication. It enables me to eliminate both my manic and depressive episodes and moderate the anti-human feeling—but does not affect the rare qualities of being Aspergian.

Of course, I remain very cautious, lonely, and single. Everywhere I go, such as restaurants, cafes, bars—I am alone. I can cope with someone talking to me, but only for a few minutes. My enthusiasm for talking to people is zero.

Because of my bipolar disorder, I never drink alcohol, coffee, or tea, and I never smoke. Years ago, alcohol was my main medicine, but it was an illusion of course. After 4–5 hours of extreme consumption, it causes a total lack of serotonin in the tanks of the brain, a stage that many people cannot deal with.

I reached this stage several times in the early era of the disorder, when I had no medication beyond alcohol. This was the medicine of the past. Of course, many people committed suicide because there was no real medicine available—and still do if they cannot access that medicine. Before I had any medicine, I resolved to commit suicide three times. However, I escaped.

The truth is that bipolar disorder can be a friendly background for developing extra ordinary talents in all areas of human activity, especially in the arts, but very few of those with bipolar disorder reach this point. The same as with Asperger's, only a very small minority make it as far as Einstein, perhaps two or three in a century. Despite this, many people with Asperger's and bipolar disorder can reach great heights in their areas of human activity without needing to reach Einstein's level.

In summary, do not allow yourself to be treated like an animal, or animal meat, by doctors. If you are diagnosed with a disorder, get a second opinion, and even a third, as doctors sometimes label people with the wrong diagnosis. Not intentionally of course, as doctors are not swindlers. It is something simpler; they are often clueless generalists who fail to understand the peculiarities of every individual.

You know your body and your mind best, so do your own research if you are diagnosed with any disorder. Find the medication or treatment that works best for you as an individual. Understand your body and mind, because it is the vessel that must sail you through this entire human life.

Fundamental Principle 5 – The continuous study of the behaviour of nature

I have been studying natural phenomena for as long I can remember, and starting now, I encourage you to also study the laws and behaviour of nature on a daily basis. You cannot function outside the scope of this principle. Your systematic engagement with the behaviour of nature during your stay in the mortal realm is a prerequisite to understanding your future mission. Remember, it is never too late to start studying books, articles, and scientific papers, as I do every day, and following the self-taught, bottom-up method of learning.

At the beginning, just like with economics, you have to get a basic education, which means becoming familiar with the known laws of nature, the content of these laws, their interactions, their results, and all of the known theoretical models about nature. However, this research should be done without accepting anything as automatically, undeniably true.

In the mortal realm we live in, we can see that there is nothing immortal, and thus, there are no immortal theories. As such, your studies of the behaviour of nature must not be done with religious adherence to "immortal" theories or the names of the wise who once said that something must be so. Your studies should be done from the bottom up, not from the top down. This means that you need neither teachers nor geniuses to learn (though by listening to them, you will also become aware of what others believe to be true).

Understand that scientists do not own nature; they are not even the main shareholders. The shareholders of nature are all the people of the world, regardless of their specialisation. This right has not been conferred on any specific scientist, association of scientists, or academic, despite some members of the scientific and academic community presenting themselves as the wisest men in the universe. Do not acknowledge anyone who calls themselves a "wise man or woman". Let them spread their "wisdom" wherever they are taken seriously, but certainly not to you.

At the same time, always be open to fresh ideas and new theories about the universe from the bright minds abundant among the ranks of scientists. There is rich talent among the newer generations of scientists, but there is an unspoken fear that their ideas will be rejected by the incumbent "rulers" who believe they have "solved" everything.

Unfortunately, most extremely talented scientists will never be heard because they run into the impenetrable walls that protect the established models. Instead, we must open the door and invite such bright minds to present themselves. We must say "the world is waiting for you; we respect you, we love you, and we want you to share your new theories with us. There is no reason to hide."

Like those fresh, bright minds, you too have to face the walls that protect the interests of those in charge. The main sponsors of these walls are the media: news stations, newspapers, and some publishers. Make no mistake, the media makes huge profits from luring us in with their offerings, encouraging us to buy books by "geniuses" or watch interviews with them, or else risk missing out on their knowledge. I strongly urge you not to buy such books. Be selective in your education.

On your journey, keep in your mind that there are no impregnable castles; all castles exist to be conquered. There are no icons or geniuses, no humans who know everything. If you blindly follow supposed icons or geniuses, you will not make any progress. The establishment will try to deceive you by claiming that the views of scientists or "geniuses" of old are sacred and immortal. Give them the answer that Jesus gave the devil when he tried to seduce Jesus toward materialistic riches: "Get away!".

Find your own answers in life. Stay away from ideologies. And always keep logic as your primary compass and your criteria to reject the ridiculous claims and theories that you encounter.

The shield of patience

In addition to a basic education, the bottom-up learning method, and a mind open to new ideas, you also need patience.

Patience is one of the key principles in life, but it is not a separate principle (such as the sixth principle, or even the first) because it is a *prerequisite* for all of the fundamental principles that guide your journey here in mortality. Patience is a universal value and acts as the connective tissue between all of the fundamental principles. Without patience, there is nothing. Everything, including your existence, will be invalid unless you carry the shield of patience.

Your search for the truth will last for as long as you are here in the mortal realm. You will not find answers easily, and you should not be disappointed if you fail to find them. This is not a negative thing. When people think they know everything, they are simply living in a glass tank of illusions, ignoring the existence of other things outside the tank. Like a goldfish.

With the passing of decades, your patient search, and your continued communication with the Supreme Beings—your companion on this journey—you will discover many new concepts through the Spontaneous Forces. This knowledge will make you wiser than any established scientist. Your wisdom will not only encourage you to reject the existing cosmological models and build new models, but it will also give you the privilege of a new perspective on the behaviour of nature.

Hold your shield of patience firmly, for you will need it on your quest to gain this knowledge, perspective, and understanding.

The danger of ideological pitfalls

On humanity's quest for new knowledge and an improved understanding of the universe and nature, mainstream science has unfortunately fallen into ideological pitfalls. As a result, many scientists' minds are religiously devoted to theories they have concluded as being true and verifiable, but only in their minds. Imagine how many potential ideas we might ignore by taking this approach. Yet, these people insist on the validity of a theory with grandiloquence and supposed proof, despite the absence of such proof in the physical world.

I must clarify that I am not a science denier by any means. In fact, I am the original product of the scientific and technological developments of the 21st century. I am a living miracle thanks to the developments of the modern era. Without these developments, I would not be here writing this book—and moreover, this book would not have been published in any past era. However, I am certainly a denier of creationism in science, ideologies in science, and religion in science.

"How can there be religion, ideologies, and creationism in science?" you are probably wondering. Well, let us consider the widely accepted Big Bang Theory. We are told by scientists that the Big Bang Theory and the theory of cosmic inflation have both been proved. The man on the street takes it for granted that the Big Bang happened. But do we have enough evidence to prove it?

The Big Bang Theory is widely accepted as one of the foundations of modern cosmology in mainstream science, and it is considered "proven" through observations. However, these observations might well have been mistaken. Despite what some scientists will have us believe, there is no unified theory of gravity and the three natural forces to support such a model. Gravity remains an unsolved mystery, one that mainstream science has considered solved since Newton's mathematics models on classical gravity and Einstein's mathematics model on general relativity. Yet both of these titans of physics may be wrong.

As you know, maths does not discover the truth. Maths is where you decide to place the truth. Maths solves problems within the box you place the problem in. It solves problems within the box of nothing more than our minds, and so it ignores an infinite number of other boxes. Maths solves a problem in one box, then science claims that this solution applies universally to the infinite number of other boxes—the existence of which was totally ignored while solving the initial problem. It is a scientific fairy-tale. Maths is by its very nature anthropic, that is, a human creation, and therefore it cannot be the means to solve problems bigger than humans.

The function of maths is to explore the results and implications of a given set of assumptions and data. If you change your assumptions or input new data, the mathematical implications change. In the case of theoretical physics, a mathematical model is a framework to understand how the underlying physics works. But it needs to be proven through physical experimentation. Otherwise, it is built on assumptions and has no relation to the real world. If your assumptions are wrong, the whole model collapses like a house of cards.

I propose a new thesis. I have a mentor in Astrophysics, Peter Jackson, who is a member of the Royal Astronomical Society, a very open-horizon society with no superiority complex, and with some accepted members as young as 18 years old. When I say that he is my mentor, I mean that I choose to read all of his scientific papers, and I learn, learn, learn every day from his wisdom. I am grateful to Peter.

When I kindly asked him to read this paper and provide feedback, he said, "It looks okay to me, though most with a physics background would dismiss it as 'unscientific waffle' or similar." Thus, I inform the physics backgrounders that I am self-taught, as I have made clear through the pages of this book, and I do not need the permission or approval of any mainstream scientist to write this or any other paper. Instead, I offer you the thoughts of Peter Jackson as feedback on my non-scientific paper:

> "We're locked into a culture where only maths and predicting 'effects' matters. So advancement of theoretical understanding stopped 50 years ago. That happened when Feynman declared it was 'too hard' to rationally understand QM (I show it wasn't, just complicated as we used false assumptions). He then picked up on Mermin's dismissal of the 'shut up and calculate' approach and turned it into a religion! That was his teacher's fault for sitting him in a corner with a calculus book when he couldn't answer his questions.
>
> But I think the key issue is 'cognitive dissonance'. i.e. When taught nonsense we embed it, and then there's no room for truth... Cognitive dissonance also has a more 'complete' definition about holding two conflicting beliefs at once."

— Peter Jackson

So, in this book, I introduce my discovery of one of the living giants of modern science, my mentor Peter Jackson. Back in 2001, the *Sunday Times* called Thales of Miletus a "Mathematician, Philosopher, Astronomer, and Merchant." Now, I offer this title to the Thales of Miletus of the 21st century, Peter Jackson—*Mathematician, Astronomer, Physicist, Philosopher, and Merchant.*

The fantasy of science

With this understanding of the universe, we can clearly see that the nature of gravity is an unsolved mystery. According to mainstream science, during what is known as "the Planck Era" (the supposed earliest stage of the Big Bang, which for me is a fantasy era that never existed), the whole universe started out smaller than a proton. In that phase, gravity was unified with the three basic forces of nature: nuclear weak force, nuclear strong force, and electromagnetism—making a single "super" force.

Many scientists believe in—and attempt to prove true—theories that whimsically combine all four forces; theories such as supersymmetry, superstrings, or supergravity. All are illusions, of course. Some superstring theories suggest that space-time had 11 dimensions during the Planck Era. Some scientists, Steven Hawking included, call the combined force theory the "Theory of Everything" or "M theory". What a fallacy. Science fiction instead of science! M theory is the theory of madness in science. The solution to everything without any evidence at all.

You see, there is no such proven theory. We simply do not know what the universe was like in the Planck Era—if such an era even existed. Yet mainstream science claims a fact from this thing that we cannot prove. There is no evidence that gravity was once unified with the three forces into a single super-force. It is merely a belief, opinion versus opinion. There is no "Theory of Everything". There is no theory of quantum gravity. There is no evidence that the genesis of the universe was a quantum event.

These theories are simply creationist formulas from scientists that from a hopeless dream strive to prove what is doomed never to be proved. Thus, the Big Bang Theory collapses from the very first moment. Perhaps we should call it "the Big Bust". This creationist approach to science is the most extreme, illogical, and mad version of reductionism.

Perhaps this all sounds shocking to you considering that the Big Bang Theory is so widely accepted? Perhaps you even assumed it was true? That being the case, bear in mind the words of James Peebles, respected cosmologist and winner of the 2019 Nobel prize in Physics. Peebles argues against the notion that the Big Bang Theory is proven, stating:

"We have no good theory of such a thing as the beginning ... We don't have a strong test of what happened ... We have theories, but not tested. ... Theories, ideas are wonderful, but to me, they become established when passing tests. ... Any bright physicist can make up theories. They could have nothing to do with reality. ... You discover which theories are close to reality by comparing to experiments. We just don't have experimental evidence of what happened."[30]

Do you still think that the Big Bang Theory is true?

The cosmic inflation challenge

In their desperate effort to fix the gap between the universe and the Big Bang Theory, scientists "discovered" another model called cosmic inflation. This theory suggests that the very early universe expanded exponentially quickly before the expansion phase began, but only for a fraction of a second.

Unfortunately for these theorists, the model of cosmic inflation faces major challenges within the scientific community. Although it is accepted as "the best option" by mainstream science, there are many voices who have spoken out against it. From time to time, scientists try to present evidence of cosmic inflation, but they fail to convince anyone other than themselves. As Peebles has said, "It's a beautiful theory... Many people think it's so beautiful that it's surely right. But the evidence of it is very sparse."

As such, we can see that mainstream science has been downgraded to creationism, and it never *discovers* anything. Scientists create evidence, but they never *discover* evidence. What scientists observe are not new discoveries but the creation of evidence to match their models.

To fix the boson missing from their cosmological model, which is known as the Standard Model, scientists created the Higgs boson. In other cases, scientists created gravitational waves and the mythological boson called "graviton". The creationists of science created gravitational waves, but even *now*, we do not know the actual nature of gravity.

Scientists say that "the Cosmic Microwave", which is a supposed remnant of the Big Bang, is evidence of the reality of the Big Bang Theory. However, this merely solves the space within one box while ignoring countless other boxes because it ignores the very existence of such boxes! When you look backwards at a distance of 13.7 billion years (science's estimated age of the universe, which may change at any moment because of new data and observations), it is impossible to compose the route with safety and confidence because there are countless unsolved boxes in the history of the universe, with 13.7 billion years of universal cataclysmic events unknown to science. Countless unseen fact-boxes exist on the path backwards, but scientists totally ignore their existence.

It is like a fisherman fishing from his boat near the beach. All of a sudden, a wave current hits his boat, and from this event and his observation of the waves' current, he suggests with confidence that he just discovered the fate and the origin of the oceans. This is exactly what scientists are doing when they create evidence. They are fishermen in a small boat near the beach, looking to solve the nature, the age, the fate, and the destiny of the oceans.

As Peebles says, "the line between what is considered completely crazy and what is considered mainstream science is constantly shifting." I call on any scientists who disagree with this blind mainstream acceptance, like Peebles, to rebel. I call forth this generation of brilliant scientists to swim to the surface and crush the old establishment. Your search begins where ideologies end.

Applying the five fundamental principles

So, now you know the five fundamental principles to pass the evolutionary exam and gain entrance to the conscious realms. You must apply these principles on a daily basis in your life on Earth. The application of these principles may sound complex for human minds, but it is achievable.

The first fundamental principle is: communication as the supreme form of meditation. This means understanding that you are not some arbitrary creation of nature, then performing daily meditation on a consistent basis to communicate with the Supreme Beings who watch over us, receiving their packages of intelligence that will help us to evolve.

The second principle is: liberation from the idolatry of the present civilisation. In short, stop wasting your time worshipping idols such as television, sports, and celebrities. Stop hunting for fame, money, and material possessions. They do not appear when you hunt them but from attracting the Spontaneous Forces into your life through communicating with the Supreme Beings. As these things have no value beyond illusion, manage them through charity to those who are deserving of it.

The third principle is: self-reliance and a frugal lifestyle free from debt. You are shackled in life by debt, by a lack of financial freedom. To resolve this, get a basic understanding of economic models and finance. Observe economic behaviours first-hand and teach yourself using the bottom-up method. Avoid banks, loans, and debt where possible. To be self-sufficient and financially self-reliant, you should live a simple and natural life, always consume less than what you produce, and always have stock of resources for emergency situations.

The fourth principle is: self-awareness to know yourself, your body, and your true nature. Have the self-confidence to know when you are the most capable of achieving something and when somebody else is better suited to the task at hand—and ask the Spontaneous Forces for guidance to find these people.

The fifth principle is: the continuous study of the behaviour of nature. As before, get a basic education in nature through bottom-up studying. Understand that there are no immortal theories or geniuses. Instead, keep an open mind and find your own answers in life. Stay away from ideologies. Always keep logic as your primary compass and your criteria for truth. Hold firm your shield of patience on your journey.

However, the fundamental principles should not be applied individually or independently of each other. They are valid and applicable to your presence here in the mortal realm only when they are all in place. This means that you will gradually build a personality that incorporates the five principles as a whole in your DNA. Therefore, you can face everything in the mortal realm from a position of strength and confidence.

PART 3

THE CONSCIOUS REALMS

Chapter 6

MY BACKGROUND AUTHORITY

Some may ask what authority I have to support my arguments in this book and to reject the evidence that scientists claim they have to support their models, especially cosmological ones. Well, my background authority is new, and it is appearing for the first time in this book. In this chapter, you will see my background authority and get a deeper understanding of the universe.

What is this background? Well, my background is the world we live in: the people, the beliefs, the behaviours, the attitudes, the social customs and morals, the democracies, the religions, the government governed through the power of money, the result of the government—expendable humanity, the anarchy, the chaos of crime, and the destruction of the natural environment. It is people's absolute beliefs that this phase of mortal reality and every phase in the past is the only form of living and that nothing follows. It is also the matter of this world, the particles, and the physical constants—the natural forces, and the scientific models, which are in a primitive and unevolved state.

In one of my great moments, not too long ago, I rejected this background and a new concept appeared in front of me. I thought: *What am I doing here with these people? Who are they, and what went wrong that I am forced to be one of them?* Then I realised I was in trouble again. I started to think about the options before me. To drink every day from morning to night until I die? No, because my DNA does not like alcohol. I drank when I was young to "cure" my depression. Now, there is no chance for me to drink alcohol; even the smell of it makes me nauseous. My other option was to become like these people. Impossible. I could not afford such contradictions against my esoteric world.

Instead, I asked for support from the Spontaneous Forces. The revelation I received from them pushed me to search for the higher worlds. I decided once and for all that I am a foreigner here in this realm of mortality. I do not belong to this world. What is happening every day on this planet is my background to reject. Its beliefs, behaviours, customs, and ethics are my background to reject.

As a result of this discovery, I absolutely rejected the mortal realm as definite and as my only stage of life. I absolutely rejected this background as an illusion. I rejected the giant illusion that other people accept—that this phase of the mortal realm is the ultimate, precious, and only stage.

By rejecting these epic illusions with absolute confidence, I gained the background authority to start searching for bigger things. On this search, I discovered the conscious realms, the Supreme Beings, the residents of the conscious realms, the higher laws of nature, the intelligent matter, the higher logic, the higher intelligence, and the higher consciousness. All of these unified as the Grand Theory of Everything in the Temple of Consciousness where the glorious Society of Composers live (which you will learn about later in this chapter).

This is my background authority, and it is the pillar of my beliefs presented everywhere in this book. The world we live in is not enough to satisfy me, nor does it match my personality or my esoteric cosmos.

For me, this background authority is real and strong—stronger than any scientific model where evidence is created to fit the theory. Ironically, scientists use the term "creationists" to describe people who disagree with their models, while at the same time creating evidence to match their fantasies. Then they claim to the people of the world that everything is solved and proved by observation and "evidence" that those very people cannot experience for themselves.

Unlike the Big Bang or cosmic inflation, this background is yours to experience. There is no need to take someone else's word for it. You may observe this background for yourself. You may reject it for yourself. You may discover your own evidence. You may open your mind to new experiences. So, I gift this background world to you; "enjoy" the chaos that it produces.

While I reject this background, I am also grateful to people—it is their attitudes that pushed me to build this background authority, to understand what they are, what I am while living in the same mortal realm as them, and why I am here but not elsewhere. Their contribution has been vital, and I can now continue my journey by presenting humans as good contributors to the higher forms of intelligence and consciousness.

The nature of consciousness

As an observer of nature, you must understand the nature of consciousness. Let us say we live inside my universe, which is a box. Because we are inside, it is impossible to see whether there are other universe-boxes out there. However, an outsider may be able to see multiple universe-boxes, either next to each other or far apart, either communicating with each other or not.

The outside observer must be a higher form of intelligence than my box because they can see more than I can. Only a very ambitious and anti-conformist inhabitant of the box may be able to break its boundaries and overcome the conditions of being an inhabitant. They may realise that the other boxes are built using different material and governed by different laws of physics. This is the conscious realm, our pair universe, as you learned in the first fundamental principle.

I argue that the conscious realm must necessarily exist because consciousness derives from there. It does not belong to the material universe, where we reside. It is a gift for us, a spark of hope.

Remember that the conscious realm is the universe where evolved matter resides? Well, we live on Earth, the material universe, the world of matter. The known material of Earth has properties that we can discover through the anthropic principles. All the laws of nature are anthropic, and the material universe is anthropic because it cannot be any different than what it is.

However, known matter is not the only form of matter, just as our known universe is not the only universe. There is evolved matter, and there is the conscious realms. Unfortunately, the vast majority of humans only perceive one world, one universe, and one kind of matter. This is because they are untrained in communication with the Supreme Beings and are completely cut off from the conscious realms.

Thankfully, all the laws of the conscious realms may be comprehensible to us if they adhere to the most powerful law—logical observation. As humans, we are just a step above animals because we developed the spark of consciousness and the compass of logic. Logic means that we may successfully navigate the mortal realm, which we are travellers in.

Upon our arrival on Earth, we are utterly devoid of both knowledge and consciousness. Through our time on Earth, we may develop this knowledge and turn our spark of implanted consciousness into a blaze. The full development of our consciousness is the crowning achievement of our searches in the depths of our mind. In this way, we can understand that the Earth has a cosmic utility; it is part of a plan among all the cosmic plans for all the universes.

The nature of animals

When you investigate the behaviour of nature, the culmination of your discoveries will be self-determination and self-awareness. This occurs only when you reach full maturity, and it emerges spontaneously after decades. It is not something that you should seek immediately.

When you have attained full maturity on Earth and have developed true self-awareness, you will know that you did not create either animals or nature. You are not the composer. Since there are things lower than you—animals and nature—there will inevitably be things higher and greater than you as well. Since you did not create these lower beings, someone else must have; otherwise, you would be sovereign over all of creation!

You will also know that you are different from animals yet similar to them. You will see for yourself that we are just a step above animals because we developed logic and a spark of consciousness. Animals developed neither logic nor intelligence. Thus, they do not evolve—they adjust to their environment through natural selection.

You will also realise that one day, animals may reach our level and become rulers of the mortal realm. I firmly believe that pets (particularly dogs and cats) will be the next animals to gain consciousness, or that they have already done so and their consciousness is evolving elsewhere in space-time.

When observed, the emotional relationship that humans share with their pets is truly amazing. The love and dedication shown by pets toward the humans who take care of them is impressive and almost inexplicable. You have no doubt known people who were so emotionally attached to their pets that when they lost them suddenly, it was as if they lost their light, the most precious companion in their life.

I urge people who love animals, especially dogs and cats, to continue doing so. In this way, you contribute greatly to the cosmic plans by training the next animal to develop consciousness. Perhaps, in an alternate universe, it is the dog and not the human who is in charge. There, dogs may keep humans who lack consciousness as their beloved pets. There, tailless dogs standing on two legs may rule and build cultures—and man may be their favourite pet.

But back to this universe, and back to your nature. When you reach full maturity, you will understand that perfect self-knowledge is not possible for mortals. It is not possible in the mortal realm. Thankfully, it is embedded in your subconscious that mortality is not the beginning nor the end of knowledge. Your knowledge will stay with you as you move through the universes.

After the length of a life in two or three universes, your prize will be reaching the pinnacle. Here, you may almost touch the conscious realms while you are still in the mortal realm. Nobel Prizes, awards, and distinctions from the unenlightened people of the mortal realm will no longer interest you. Your prize will be entry into the conscious realms, where the Supreme Beings will judge your harvest in the mortal realm and perhaps reward you with a new incarnation as a more evolved being.

The path of success

So, mortality is not the end, although humans perceive it as such. On this Earth, when our hour of departure from this mortal realm comes, it is referred to by the very inhumane word "death". For those of us who succeed, who evolve, our mortal departure means leaving behind human concepts such as time and death.

For the few of us (or even the one) who succeed in passing the evolutionary exams, time and death will cease to exist. In the laws of evolution, we will transition to higher space-time fields. There, time functions either as a friend or as a spectator—it has no essential role in our activities as it does here on Earth. It causes no wear and tear with its passage as it does here.

However, when we—the evolved few—eventually depart the mortal realms, we do not abandon our consciousness here on Earth. In fact, the exact opposite happens—the consciousness abandons the matter. Upon our arrival in the conscious realms, we are not stripped of knowledge or consciousness. On the contrary, we carry with us the baggage of knowledge and experience.

In the conscious realms, consciousness does not start from scratch as it does here on Earth. Rather, we begin a new journey with full awareness of every experience gained from the turbulent, violent, and hostile prison we have escaped from. However, we understand that the most violent features of mortality are considered useful because they trained our consciousness. We also appreciate that in the conscious realms, our "incarnation" means removing the awful shackles that we experienced in the mortal realm such as time, damage, accidents, illnesses, and death.

In the conscious realms, we are not trapped in material bodies of known matter, like in the mortal realms. The next highest form of known matter is "evolutionary matter", named in accordance with the concept of natural evolvement.

Your new body, which is made of particles of evolved matter, is your subordinate and not your master. It does not need food in way we understand; it does not decay, nor age, nor fall ill, and it does not weaken. On the contrary, it travels wherever you command it to and it takes whatever form you desire. It can take you to any point in space-time, and you can relive all of your experiences on planet Earth as you wish and in any setting.

The theory of time and evolution

Let us consider time in more depth. The anthropic form of time is generally accepted in the mortal realms. This theory is based on the anthropic principles. The idea is that if humans were not here, no one would know that time was progressing. In other words, time does not exist except in the thoughts of human beings.

Unlike the prevailing scientific opinion, I propose a more expansive model of time: the exciting concept of unified time, which we will discuss in chapter 9. I believe that the current mainstream notion of time is primitive, and we probably carry this notion from the very early eras of Homo sapiens' existence on Earth.

Perhaps the first humanoid born on Earth reacted to space and their surroundings with their first thought, and that is how time began to flow. Thus, an initial thought that reacted to space was called time. I am open to any logical hypotheses. For now, I do not consider time a unique discovery of Earthlings, nor do I accept any single interpretation of time. My evidence for this is that we can compare the extremely brief history of humankind (approximately 6 million years) to the history of the universe (an estimated 13.7 billion years).

In the conscious realms, time cannot apply in the same way as it does on Earth, in the mortal realms. There, time is a completely different concept that has a neutral direction. But as human interpretation does not work in areas where the anthropic laws are void, we might as well forget it. Other laws exist that we cannot even comprehend because of our limited anthropic identity in this known universe.

The conscious realms are not part of the known universe. They form a conscious realm in coexistence with matter. In the conscious realms, conscious activity is governed by higher, non-anthropic laws. The material hosting consciousness is shaped by these non-anthropic laws, that is, shaped by the inhabitants of the conscious realms. Note that these laws are very different from the incomplete natural laws that have been discovered by the anthropic principles.

In the conscious realms, matter evolves and has its own intelligence. This evolved matter has enormous transformational capabilities. It creates settings for every type of intelligent life throughout the annals of time. This means that beings higher than you, Supreme

Beings, have been working systematically for billions of years to shape the settings that you receive for your training, and they have obeyed the regulatory rules. When you advance to Supreme Being level and become a regulator, you will be equipped with the precious experiences you gained in the mortal realm.

Just as our Earth is friendly to the development of intelligent life through this training, the evolved matter is friendly to the development of conscious life. In evolved matter, the particles are fractals or sparks of intelligence. As a conscious being made of evolved matter, you are far superior to your mortal form. You have an enormous mass of intelligent particles under your command, and so you can travel to any point in the universe regardless of time. With this understanding, time travel is perfectly possible. You could even decide to visit the past of the human universe, not just your own past.

To travel in time, just as in the human understanding of physics, we must discover "wormholes" in the universe. (I borrow the term "wormhole" from Einstein, who I consider to have the greatest scientific human mind.) The higher laws that bind the Supreme Beings are applied by the method of a wormhole, thus bypassing the areas of force in the natural laws.

Wormholes are a mathematical prediction of Einstein's general relativity theory. Yet, no such thing has been found anywhere in the material universe, and no such thing will be found in the near future either. For humans, a wormhole is merely a mathematical tool that we use to connect points in space-time, but as we have not discovered any, the concept belongs to science fiction rather than science.

For the Supreme Beings, wormholes are not a mathematical tool but a space-time bridge to reach us. The Supreme Beings are engineers of these wormholes, and they utilise them to connect the conscious universe with the material universe. They arrive in the mortal realms from the conscious realms through these wormholes, bypassing the natural laws and time-distance that separate the conscious universe from the material universe.

The compass of logic

As you embark on your search, always keep in mind that you have a compass to navigate the ocean of your search—logic, which is the mother of all anthropic laws. However, note that logic does not prohibit the existence of other types of logic. This means that other forms of logic exist, which were born from other sets of natural forces and may live in non-anthropic universes. We humans have our logic, but there may be logic-brothers and logic-sisters that exist elsewhere. Infinite amounts perhaps. There may be logic-children born of other logic-mothers that do not conform to the anthropic laws.

The mother of logic is consciousness. Consciousness as a colonist of human minds created the logic that we have on Earth according to the current natural laws of the anthropic universe. (Remember that consciousness arrives as a colonist in the brains of all humans during their very early years in the physical body.) However, consciousness as the original governor of the non-anthropic universe—and not a colonist of human minds—creates higher, more advanced forms of logic according to evolved matter and evolved natural laws.

As a result, there may be a universe governed by a logic-brother of ours, born from a different set of natural laws. This different set of natural laws may match those of the evolved matter and the non-anthropic conscious realm. In fact, there are no doubt many conscious realms, as there is no logical reason for there being just one.

Note that while consciousness colonises human brains as toddlers, we may invite other entities from the conscious realms to become colonists in our brains later in life. I perceive the colony as an autonomous entity that has colonised billions of brains in an amazing scattering of quantum waves, sending consciousness out across the universes.

The Temple: the Grand Theory of Everything

The Temple of Consciousness is where the Society of Composers live. Composers started out like all of us in the mortal realms, then qualified for the various levels of the conscious realms, and finally self-qualified as Temple residents.

The Composers who live in the conscious realms are infinite in number; it is inconcievable for us to imagine how many of them there are. They are the composers of all kinds of material universes and all kinds of conscious realms. They are the engineers of the evolved matter and the users of the evolved matter. They are the commanders of the evolved matter and the intelligent particles.

They can appear everywhere they wish, in all areas that consciousness lives—even here on Earth. They may travel anywhere they wish, in all areas of the realms. They may have any shape they wish, as they use the intelligent particles of their advanced matter to build any kind of physical body. They might be somewhere near us, but we will never recognise them because we are not permitted to. They can travel in time as we understand it because for them, time is unified. They experience whatever they wish as inhabitants of any of the mortal areas or conscious realms.

They are the sum of our equations, the sum of all conscious fractal bosons. They are all of us at once.

In this way, we can understand that the Society of Composers *are* the Temple, as well as living in the Temple. They are everything. The Temple is the Grand Theory of Everything. It is the composition of everything of being. It is the unification of all Spontaneous Forces, all forms of logic, all forms of intelligence. It is the sum of being everywhere and forever. It is the extreme form of power composed of *everything*.

On common ground

Now, let us return from the Temple to the common ground we stand upon. Here in the mortal realms, we develop intelligence according to the brain chemicals and brain capacities of each individual, which differ substantially. Some people—very few—are at the highest level of expanding intelligence and consciousness. These are the people who will qualify for the conscious realms after their departure from the mortal realms. They are the evolved few.

For the vast majority of people, this target is far away, too far away to even think or dream of. And for the vast majority, it is impossible to think or dream of this because they ignore the existence of anything outside their basic five senses. Thus, they ignore the existence of the conscious realms or anything beyond this mortal planet. They are so far behind in the race of intelligent evolution that they might need billions of years to catch up.

Unfortunately, the vast majority of Earthlings never spiritually evolve enough to qualify for anything higher than the mortal realms, such as Earth. In fact, they often go backwards and are forced to live again and again in even worse conditions in other mortal worlds similar to Earth because they fail to start the evolutionary process. The conscious realms are not "free entrance" areas, and nobody gets a ticket without passing the evolutionary exams.

I remind you again of the cosmic role of the mortal realms as a school to train your consciousness in the face of harsh and violent trials. This is its role, and the commandment from the conscious realms is that the mortal realms should be maintained at any cost. To preserve it, we need to ensure that the Earth will continue to be hospitable for the development of intelligent life. It is our duty to follow and serve this commandment, and I act within the framework of this commandment.

From now on, as you apply the fundamental principles in your life, disregard the constraints of time and remain strictly and infinitely focused on your task of evolving. I will watch over your efforts and strengthen you however I can. Your success is one of my personal goals. It will be a small feat of mine to see you gaze upon the conscious realms.

In order to help ourselves, we must overcome the genetic imperfections that we encounter every day as part of this realm's conditions. Personally, I fought day in and day out against wild beasts who have consciousness like me and you, but they are not equal to us. They are humans but the worst kind of animal on this Earth. Yet no one and nothing has defeated me, and nothing can bring me down. My self-confidence comes from the guidance I receive from the Spontaneous Forces. It can be yours too.

I once said that the world is lost and will destroy itself through nuclear, biological, or economic warfare. All of these scenarios are still open, and you will learn more about the true nature of this world in the next part of the book. Nothing can definitively prevent the destruction of the Earth, and violence is deeply rooted in the DNA of the world's inhabitants.

Yet on my journey, I met certain human beings who were victims of this world—without spiritual training but with good faith and willingness to embody this new knowledge. Thus, I decided to wage a final war in defence of the mortal realms, to save humans from themselves. The Spontaneous Forces agree that the mortal realms must retain their cosmic role, and they have given me the message to give to humanity.

If we succeed, the Earth will survive and continue to play its cosmic role, and you will make yourself known as a winner in the evolutionary race to move to the conscious realms. The final outcome is up to you and your efforts. Whatever the final outcome will be, those in the conscious realms will simply record it.

Are you ready to join the evolutionary way?

Chapter 7

THE EVOLUTIONARY
RACE OF INTELLIGENCE

On our Earth, it is inevitable that the evolutionary race of intelligence will take place. There is no other option. The season requires that the race be conducted. The Supreme Beings in the conscious realms decided on it. They judged that the time has come for the evolution of intelligence, which will result in mortals on Earth running the greatest race of all time. You have to be ready and fully prepared for it, because there are very few who will finish, though the reward for doing so will be unfathomably great. In other mortal realms, the race has already been run, and the winners and losers have already emerged.

The galactic capsules for experimentation

As human beings, we are terrestrials, but there is a multitude of other species with similar levels of culture—perhaps in our galaxy, another galaxy, or the galaxies of other universes. In the conscious realms, the Supreme Beings monitor the galactic differences between such civilisations. They watch solar maps of the mortal realms—technologies of the higher natural laws—to observe what is happening. (I write this parabolically because there is no other way to convey the message.)

The Supreme Beings recognise the cosmic significance of conditions and changes, including conflicts, wars, climate risks, crime rates, politics, the economy, scientific and technological developments, and inhabitants' behaviours. They understand the viability of the planets they observe based on how the inhabitants use their physical and productive resources.

This means that our planet has the significance of being a precious capsule for experimentation. We are used by those in the conscious realms to develop intelligence and consciousness, not just on our planet but in all of the mortal realms. We are not isolated from the other mortal realms, although we ignore the existence of them. On the contrary, to the Supreme Beings, we are all considered a big group of planets with similar potential for development and expansion.

These beings look at us from far away, but altogether. They hear the stories of everyday madness that are playing out on each planet and they eventually watch the capsules explode, which means the self-destruction of that civilisation. They see explosions everywhere.

The experiments of messiahs

As the mortal realms, including Earth, are a training school for consciousness, at least some of these schools must survive. This is why those in the conscious realms conduct their experiments. They observe the circumstances that we, the foolish, create. Accordingly, they decide on new experiments and trials for us. They set the experiments, then they leave us to run. As inhabitants of the mortal realms, humans participate in these cosmic experiments without realising it. We have no idea that we are participating in any kind of experiment at all, like rats or guinea pigs in a laboratory.

These experiments occur roughly every few centuries or so in human history. In these experiments, the conscious realms periodically send messages via messiahs to those on Earth and in other mortal realms. These messages are a tool, and they have the purpose of improving human DNA to create the evolution of intelligence.

Messiahs are of far less importance than some religions suggest. They are merely people like you, but with specific genetic traits. A messiah emerges from an astonishing combination of rare genetic traits. There is no specific messianic gene. A messiah's emergence also depends on the era's necessity for such a messiah.

In the course of human history, we can witness the experiments in the messages of love and light sent to humankind through the messiahs, mystics, or gurus of the past depending on the era they lived in. Likewise, we can view it in the message of this book—the race for evolutionary intelligence. After sending the message through a messiah, those in the conscious realms watch without intervening in what takes place.

Within the general population, there is only a minority of humans who can address the Supreme Beings. Among the few of us who communicate with them, there will always be pre-selected prophets—those who have the appropriate genetic material from pre-Earth life to evolve into mediators in the transmission of Supreme messages. This is true of all of the prophets, messiahs, and mystics of the past.

The unknown messiah

I am convinced that Jesus of Nazareth, whoever he was—a man with a name that is written in the *New Testament*—had this rare genetic combination. But he emerged as the unknown messiah in part because the era he lived in needed him. The era required his sacrifice to appease the low intelligence level of people at that time. His message gave humans, those who lived during his life and in subsequent generations, a method to experience spirituality, and an evolution of sorts occurred in their minds.

When the unknown messiah Jesus appeared, his society and the societies preceding it were utterly authoritarian, barbaric, and inhumane. Women had no value—they were viewed as lower than animals—and many poor people were slaves who had no rights and lived in miserable conditions.

At the time, small groups of landowners and livestock owners exercised an inhuman form of power over inferior land and livestock owners. Crowds of people born in the lower ranks were the product of rape, which was once a daily routine—a ruthless and systematic degradation of the female human being as slaves in the sexual service of any man in power.

Thus, the unknown Jesus of Nazareth came to impose new laws, new societal morals, and new perceptions. Although Jesus the man is unknown, we can conclude something about him by reading his wonderful, enchanting, and beautiful sermon that he delivered while sitting on a hill. Although the crowd did not fully grasp the details of the message, they listened with ecstasy. "The Sermon on the Mount" is one of the most beautiful examples of sound thought worldwide. It is a speech by a human messiah who gave his best to the beings

THE TEMPLE OF CONSCIOUSNESS

imprisoned within the mortal world.

In this sermon, Messianic messages of change emerged—including liberation from the bonds of time and death, and the need for love, justice, charity, simplicity, physical life, humility, polite behaviour, communication with higher beings, and a focus on the higher life that follows our present life. This was an entirely new global vision of structural thought, through which the notion of society, family, and virtue was developed in the centuries that followed.

Jesus conveyed to mankind a message of the evolution of human societies—the necessity of transitioning from the barbarity and arbitrariness of the few privileged into organised societies and states that benefitted every human being.

Although I discuss the words of Jesus in this book, we may also look to the words of other prophets, teachers, mystics, and enlightened people in the East (China and India, for example) to find similar wisdom. Humans underestimate the contribution of prophets such as Moses, Prophet Muhammad (PBUH), the Buddha, and Confucius.

All of these exceptional teachers contributed to the founding of new societies, and all are of universal significance. I respect all of these great prophets. In this book, I mostly (though not absolutely) observe and refer to the Western world, and this is why I reference Jesus from Nazareth rather than the other influential prophets.

Do you know why I write about Jesus and the other enlightened masters as inseparable? Because in the mortal realms, there is no one indivisible truth. On the contrary, there are pieces of knowledge and truth that you will discover in all religions and in all teachings. In my personal family history, the Bible and the Koran were dominant in my early religious studies and education. The Koran was my spontaneous natural selection as I feel so close to, and friendly, with Muslims.

This is because of my ancestry and homeland of Cyprus. On my father's side, neutrals; on my mother's side, Christians. Later in my life, I chose a completely personal path of communication with the Supreme Beings and to receive packages of powerful knowledge from them. I combined the virtues and truths taught by all of the prophets, messiahs, and mystics—giving them the beautiful habitat of this book, combining them into the powerful new knowledge you find here.

A new messiah

It is important to note that we are not here to admire the past; we are here to create the past, as you will learn in chapter 10. This is why a new prophet, a new messiah, must deliver powerful, new knowledge. To move further as a species, the new must abolish the old. We must find a new way, and abandon the previous way. As a result, a new prophet or messiah is always evolved in relation to the previous one. They cannot simply continue from where the previous messiah stopped. No, they must abolish the past as useless to the spiritual needs of the current phase of humanity.

Why? Because times have changed since the unknown Jesus' teachings. We are not the people who were his audience. Our needs and ambitions are fundamentally different from the poor fishermen who were Jesus' followers. We live in the era of information. As a race, we are ready and hungry to understand far wider concepts. That is why this era calls for a new messianic message, and why we as humans are prepared to witness the new message. This era calls for the message of evolution.

The routine of evolutionary races

The race for evolution may sound wonderful to us, but to a Supreme Being, it is just a routine to conduct across the mortal realms. They care not for the results of such races, no matter who wins or who loses, either here or anywhere else. For those in the conscious realms, there is no success or failure! Such notions only exist for the residents of the mortal realms. Whatever will arrive as the outcome will not cause the Supreme Beings the slightest emotional feeling. They will simply record the result.

The same applies to me. I send the message of the urge for evolution— and the purpose of the planet Earth continuing to be a living planet and a consciousness school. But I will not cry if the final result is the destruction of the planet. I will merely continue my journey elsewhere. My emotions will be neutral, and I will not celebrate if the message is successful. For me, there is no success, and no failure either.

This answers questions I have heard many times in my life from naive people, such as "Where is God?" and "Why does he never intervene?" Many people conclude that since he does not intervene, he does not exist. However, the notion of "God" commonly referred to by religions does not convey the reality of the situation.

In actuality, the tenants of the conscious realms are not the single and absolute master of creation. This is the creationistic view, which I absolutely reject. In the new model proposed in this book, Supreme Beings are a large crowd governed by the Society of Composers, who are the highest entities in the cosmic hierarchy.

As you learned earlier, these Supreme Beings use the postman of the conscious realms to deliver packages of wisdom to humans. Some religions recognise this postman by the name the "Holy Spirit". The Supreme Beings have the power to bless us and generously provide us with powerful knowledge, and to send messages. However, they do not intervene *universally* to change the course of human history.

They set the experiments and record the outcomes for all of humanity, and they help individuals who request their help, but we are the ones who create the ultimate history of our planet. We are the ones who listen to such messages or ignore them. Thus, the "Gods"—a word that I abolish as the main symbol of creationists—do not intervene because it is not their role.

The race for evolutionary intelligence

As humans, we are in the realm of free will, and it must not be restricted by higher beings. Ironically, it is humans who set limits on free will. In the 21st century, only the tenants of the Dark Rooms have true free will. What free will can billions of expendable humans possibly have? How can a poor inhabitant of the world apply free will when he is enslaved for 24 hours a day to secure a measly piece of bread for him and his family?

Make no mistake, the fact that we have annulled free will in our mortal realm does not concern those in the conscious realms. It is us who have mistakenly managed the commodity of free will. It is us who have brought "civilisation" (as I generously call it) to within a step of chaos. Those in the conscious realms do not care about the tenants of the Dark Rooms. They are ants, just like the rest of humankind. Those in the Dark Rooms hugely overestimate their importance in the cosmic scheme of things. They have pushed humankind towards chaos and extinction through their foolish actions. But there is a way to escape this fate—to win the evolutionary race of intelligence.

The outcome of the race will be a new advanced form of intelligence that will dominate the future—they will be the winners. The danger of losing the race will not turn out to be nothing. For the losers, civilisation will almost certainly disappear. Therefore, each individual must decide to evolve, as there is no other room left for them. They are doomed to die here as useless and non-evolved material unless they decide to evolve. Thus, they will be sent backwards; not backwards in time, but backwards in their personal and physical circumstances.

It is simple—either we are destroyed and identified as lost material in the universe or we succeed and win the race. However the race is run, the Supreme Beings will simply record the outcome. They will not get involved or intervene in any way to create the outcome. We are the ones who will create the outcome for ourselves. We are the Gods and the demons at the same time upon this Earth.

I have chosen to fight to the end against the demons, who are not mythical beasts from hell, but the human beings on Earth who have a destructive, negative mentality. These people, with their destructive actions and behaviours, are the true enemies of peace, harmony, and life—both physical and intelligent. If the demons defeat us, then the end of humanity will be the result.

This, of course, includes those in the Dark Rooms and those who are obedient to them: the corrupt and failed politicians, the bankers, the capitalists, and the pathetic, naive, self-interested people I meet every day. I invite you to join me in my triumphant approach, but please do not follow me; just leave me alone in my peaceful state. Fight for your own peace.

Understand that we are entering the most critical period in the history of our species as a bearer of intelligent life. To endure the difficult conditions of the race and become a victor, you must prepare adequately. You will be taking part in the battle of all battles. Your preparation requires a radical change in the way you look at the world. You need to shed your past self, just as I have shed my past self many times. You need to be ready to invite the Supreme Beings to settle in your brain.

With this radical change, you must understand that there is no ego, no one and single brain like they teach you in school. We cannot be separated from all of consciousness. This is why our brains are designed to receive the arrival of new colonists who will manage the chemistry, neurons, and information stored in there. New information will enter your mind daily in the significant areas of your brain that involve the reception of data, development, and awareness.

When you invite the Supreme Beings into your mind, you may become a victor in the evolutionary race of intelligence. It is never too late to start preparing for the race. Even if the Dark Rooms destroy this Earth and our civilisation along with it, you will continue the evolutionary race in another mortal realm—as long as you have started on the evolutionary way.

The magnetism of Ancient Egypt

With all that I have described about human beings and all that you have seen with your own eyes, you may doubt whether any humans are capable of winning the evolutionary race at all. I promise you that at least some have the potential to win the race.

An excellent example of human potential is Ancient Egypt. Personally, I am fascinated by the spirit of Ancient Egypt. Even today when I visit that magical country, I feel like I am on a pilgrimage. The ancient spirit is pervasive there, and the atmosphere is striking and mysterious. In Egypt, I feel so beautiful and familiar, as if I have lived in these places before and may declare myself an Ancient Egyptian.

Yes, I am in love with Ancient Egypt, but I also consider today's Egypt to be the most beautiful and fascinating country in the world. I invite you to visit her at least once to experience the magnetic euphoria and the imposing light of dawn before this Earth is destroyed. This light is the result of the Magnetic Arc's influence over the region of Egypt, the Middle East, and the Eastern Mediterranean. Here, great civilisations flourished and great prophets were born, even the unknown Jesus of Nazareth.

The Magnetic Arc is not a scientific discovery of course, but a spiritual, personal discovery. I found this atmosphere of the Magnetic Arc in Egypt. It is a spiritual feeling of being in high mood and top spiritual form to understand new, higher concepts than what ordinary people understand. No doubt, the Pharaohs themselves found their Magnetic Arc too.

The Egyptian pyramids are a testament to what the human brain can accomplish if it remains concentrated on and committed to its goal. Especially if it ignores the advice of "wise" scientists and supposed geniuses who think they know everything but know nothing about the essentials. For scientists, there is nothing beyond equations, observations, and proof. They work exclusively with primitive methods and mindsets, as if they were stuck in the time of Thales of Miletus, who laid the framework for natural determinism six centuries before the birth of the unknown Jesus.

If the Pharaohs had asked the experts, scientists, and academics of their time, you can be certain that there would be no pyramids today. The whole mob of fools would have answered "You're crazy. Those things don't happen. You're arrogant if you think you can build that." Fortunately, the Pharaohs did not ask every fool. They were the owners of the Earth. So they proceeded to accomplish their noble tasks with complete confidence in the final result.

Some people believe that the Egyptian pyramids are miracles, but remember that the laws of nature **always** apply. It is impossible to suspend the force of natural laws. While the Pyramids receive a multitude of speculators and conspiracy theorists (who suggest they were made by extra-terrestrials, for example), I firmly believe that they are the work of the Ancient Egyptian Pharaohs and their extraordinary engineers. Ancient Egyptian engineers had incredible mechanical skills.

The pyramids are no miracle. These top symbols of the world were created by the Pharaohs and their brilliant engineers under the direction of those in the conscious realms. The directions were placed in their brains through the method of a spiritual wormhole, which is not a breach of the natural laws.

Understand that the higher laws are imposed on the known natural laws, but they do not nullify them, nor do they suspend them. Higher laws are not even *close* to known laws. They apply simultaneously and independently. Yet, at the absurd request of religions, they want us to accept that the violation of natural laws is possible, or at least that the power of natural laws is deferred. I respond to this with the weapon of logic. Of course there are natural laws that have not been discovered. There are also higher laws that apply to advanced matter in the fields of space-time.

The application of higher laws is the transfer of powerful knowledge to those who regularly engage in communication with the Supreme Beings. In some cases, this powerful knowledge will create the potential for an outcome that *looks like* a miracle, such as the Egyptian pyramids. It is also possible that this powerful knowledge can cure diseases such as alcoholism and even "incurable" diseases such as cancer. Nevertheless, this procedure neither infringes nor suspends the force of natural laws.

With this understanding, we can reconsider the concept of miracles. Miracles are an exploration of the hidden powers of the brain. A miracle is the discovery of these hidden forces and properties—and the process of their emergence from the depths of our mind to the surface. A miracle is therefore the discovery of new, astonishing properties of the brain to achieve incredible feats.

The cosmic plans

Aside from being architectural wonders, the Pyramids are the best memorials of the cosmic plans for intelligent life on our planet. The Composers of the universes sent those Pharaohs on a journey to build them, just like the Composers sent me with a message for humanity. They gifted me and (all humans) with consciousness and logic. They commanded me to "begin work", and so I became the collector of experiences and consciousness, with a starting point similar to the base of a pyramid. Thus, I start in a different direction from the whole spectrum of the base, and I continue my experience of upward consciousness until I become one with the Composers.

As depicted in the design of the Great Pyramids, the vast majority of humans are at the base; they are simple forms of intelligence. The purpose of human presence here is the collection of experiences and the greatest possible evolution to raise the level of consciousness. It is the cosmic plans.

However, each person takes a different position in the pyramid due to the different chemical properties of their brain, level of evolvement, and previous spiritual battles in other mortal realms. We are together here, but we are not the same. We are all fighters, but the battles we take part in have many varying difficulty levels. My battles are different from yours, dear friend.

My battle is that I was chosen to carry the message to you, and to be a successful messenger, I had to live in the most complicated, difficult, and unthinkable personal circumstances. I had to be sacrificed for you, not just for two days like the unknown Jesus suffered (according to the *New Testament*), but for as long as my whole presence in the mortal realms lasts. Thus, please never judge the current conditions of my life or anybody else's life, because our battles are different.

This explains why the Ancient Pharaohs and their exceptional engineers were substantially different from modern man. The difference was in how their brains worked. This enabled them to build Ancient Egypt, with a wealth of marvellous works beyond the Pyramids.

These days, modern humans do not believe in the dynamics and properties of the brain that were elected in the cosmic plan. Contemporary people do not believe in the higher powers of the brain because they fail to recognise them. And they fail to recognise them because they believe that all sorts of self-professed experts and scientists know more about them than they know about themselves! The knowledge is there, but they cannot see it, because they do not trust their minds to search for it and seek it!

Do you believe that everyone who self-promotes as an expert or a scientist is infallible? Do you take all of the gibberish that you hear seriously? Do you berate your own abilities so much?

I invite you to transform yourself into an Ancient Egyptian Pharaoh as far as your mindset is concerned. In these titans, there is the secret of self-confidence as a result of self-knowledge. I had to discover it, and to do so, I had to fight like a lion against the monsters of the established mentality and established education. You too can fight like a lion against the binds of Western civilisation. You can win the race of evolution.

WE-I-ONE

To win the race, you must analyse and study the burden of consciousness. The first question you must ask yourself is: do I know anything about the nature of consciousness? Some think that they know. Others think it is so simple that it is not worth their time. Some think they can solve it easily, but they always fail at the last minute.

All of these people make the same mistake. They think that consciousness is a creation, development, or evolution of the human brain. They have never conceived of the possibility that consciousness is colonised in the brain. You learned the beautiful concept of the origin of consciousness in chapter 1. Now let us go further and deeper.

Because of the burden of consciousness, the ability to think surprisingly develops. The result of the functioning of the conscious brain is an enormous ocean of thoughts. At the same time, however, consciousness sets the limits of deterrence, which are given the beautiful name "logic".

This is the differentiation between Homo sapiens and other animals. You were the animal chosen to host consciousness in your brain, and consciousness sets the foundation for logic. Logic cannot operate in any other way than a deterrent. Socrates spoke of a "deterrent demon" who must rule the world of beings.

Logic often applies to what *not* to do, although it also applies to *what* to do. For example, do not rape women, because you are not like the other animals; do not kill people, do not be arrogant, do not act against the interests of the others, do not occupy land that belongs to others, do not cheat others, do not sell yourself for small things. Yet, it is also logical to look after your body because it must get you through this life, to act in the interest of others, to be humble, and so on.

Consciousness is your compass to successfully navigate the ocean of thoughts, and while you are on the journey, it triggers the emergence of certain properties in your brain. The chemistry of the brain also determines the characteristics of each property. This explains why we are all different from one another. We are fractal bosons of consciousness and independent entities at the same time.

Because we are all different in terms of our brain chemistry, this is what makes Earth a good training ground for consciousness. It also helps that our training is conducted in the harshest conditions of the violent prison that biologists call life. According to biologists, we are almost genetic clones. This is right. But it is not enough. The most striking thing is that we are *conscious* clones.

This may sound paradoxical, but that is the nature of consciousness— it is endless. Because of the nature of consciousness, we are at the same time both ourselves and all the others. We are us and everyone else simultaneously. Both now and in the past. We have always existed in the past as other people. We have known the biological end of life maybe hundreds of times. This means that I am me, I am you, I am everybody who lives now, everybody who lived before, and everybody who will live after, either in this mortal realm or in any other mortal realm.

The WE-I-ONE doctrine is based on the non-anthropic nature of consciousness, and it means that nothing is consciously isolated. It also means that all bearers of consciousness—all humans on this Earth—are bound together in a very distinct relationship—one of a quantum entanglement function, differentiated by the individual chemical compositions of our brains.

Thus, we must all act and achieve the results both as a whole and independently at the same time. We should not be introverts, provincials, or like the scientists. Let us put aside unnecessary selfishness. The "I" has decayed.We are accountable to the Supreme Beings in both of our capacities, as a whole and as fractal bosons.

Yet on our departure from the planet, any link with our mortal realm is cancelled, our entanglement relationship to other humans is severed. At this stage, we are in the area of transition—the area between the mortal realms and the conscious realms, where the Supreme Beings will decide on the next phase of colonisation for each individual. Hereafter, there is no relationship or contact between us and our former species any longer. The final path of consciousness is not our problem.

We who are here are called to meet now in the final days. Otherwise, self-destruction is our fateful future, as has happened to other colonies of consciousness in the universe before us. We are called to tear ourselves from the animals, who we inexplicably insist on behaving like, yet claim that we are superior to.

Let us leave the animals in their privacy. Animals are the indigenous inhabitants of the Earth. We are all aliens, travellers in the realm of mortality. Our behaviours are a danger to these indigenous creatures, and we are threatening them with extinction. Indeed, the whole Earth is in danger because of our presence here. No, the animals must survive! It is us who are commanded to evolve and to re-invent our lives. So, I invite you fractal bosons of consciousness to re-invent your life and start the evolutionary race of intelligence.

Why, you might be wondering, is the race of evolution only happening on Earth right now? Why has it taken so long? Simply put, it could not have happened at any other time in human history. In the past, messiahs, prophets, mystics, and teachers came to send us messages of love, light, nirvana, and progress, because that is what the era permitted and required. Only now when humans are able to evolve is it possible for people to receive the message of evolution.

Until now, nobody on Earth was aware of the need to evolve. The Earth required 4.5 billion years to reach this level, and humans required 6 million years of existence to reach this level. Make no mistake, we have reached this level due to cataclysmic developments in technology and science. As I explained, without such developments, I would have died from depression and alcoholism very early in life.

Only in the year 2020 did Earth become a friendly enough planet to allow the development and the evolution of intelligence. For all of these reasons, I am here now, as the carrier of the message for the race of evolution. And only now are you able to hear it.

Chapter 8

THE NON-ANTHROPIC PRINCIPLE

The whole global structure of Western civilisation (a civilisation that is going through its final days, in my model of observation) has two foundations: the Ancient Greek school of thought and Christianity. These two strong foundations contributed ideologically to the formation of the Western culture we see today. Both are the products of selective, even arbitrary interpretations depending on the circumstances at the time—and what was most agreeable to the aspirations of those with authority.

You learned about the foundation of Christianity in the previous chapter. It is also important to understand the foundation of Ancient Greece, as Ancient Greek thought is the strong foundation of modern science, in order to pave a new way forward.

The foundation of modern science

Ancient Greek thought has two basic pillars: **scientific determinism** and **reductionism**. Scientific determinism as an idea was introduced by the natural philosophers of Ionia—initially by Thales of Miletus. The pre-Socratic Ionian philosophers who continued these ideas were mostly Thales' students, such as Anaximander, and later Socrates and his student Plato.

These philosophers introduced the anthropic principles based on the Thales' initial idea; he conceived of using structural thought when observing natural phenomena. Despite this, our current scientists place the birth of the anthropic principles in the 20th century. What a joke!

By combining the observation of nature through structural thought—and connecting physical determinism and the anthropic principles—reductionism emerged as a tool of applied relationships in nature. This is one of the pillars of modern science. Other pillars include quantum mechanics (a genuine example of how reductionism applies) and general relativity, both of which derive from the natural determinism and anthropic principle of the Ionians.

In Plato's great work the *Timaeus* dialogue, he asserted that man recognises order in the universe, not disorder and disintegration. Man is the one who places himself in the position of an observer and curator responsible for the order and virtue of the universe. Without man, there would be no order, no virtue, no laws in the universe, but an eternal and unending process of dissolution and chaos.

This is the most beautiful interpretation of the anthropic principles. Of course, before the Ionians, the Egyptians introduced structural thought in the field of personal development, which is why they were able to create the pyramids and other monuments. Yet, this idea does not apply anymore, so we can consider it terminated. It served for many centuries—making the most of observation, the discovery of laws, and order in the universe. But now, it is time for new, non-anthropic principles to take humankind forward.

For the first time ever, someone is asking for you to overcome your anthropic nature. Why? Because it is possible! The one who asks this from you has already succeeded. You can also achieve this if you follow the evolutionary way. Dare to think about. Dare to overcome the world and its anthropic nature.

The anthropic principles

Despite the anthropic principles first flowing from Ancient Egypt and Greece, modern scientists have their own version of the anthropic principles, which were formed in the 20th century. According to the anthropic principles of scientists, you and I exist—moreover, the universe exists—as a result of an agreement between the forces of nature, the physical constants, and the laws of chemistry and biology.

The 20th century anthropic principles are the perfect unobtrusive conspiracy. Our supposed forefathers, who are the forces of nature, the physical constants, and the chemical and electric constants, did not allow the slightest divergence from that which is true and that which we observe to be true. In other words, they argued that something is true because we observe it to be true, and if it were not true, we would not be able to observe it because we would not exist to observe it!

Their argument is that any divergence, albeit a negligible differentiation in physical constants, would prohibit the creation of galaxies, stars, solar systems, and planets—much less a friendly environment for the creation of life and intelligent life, such as we observe and know applies here on our planet.

Although such principles are mildly accepted within the scientific community, there are still many battles and arguments between the scientists who favour the anthropic principles and those who reject them. From the plethora of forms of anthropic principles, the most logical form is structural thought in the observation of natural phenomena, which was first introduced by Thales and the Ionians, then presented in this book as an essential pillar of human evolution.

The opportunity arises

The vast majority of the inhabitants of our mortal realm squander their lives here. However, they will all have many opportunities in other mortal realms to evolve and reach the higher, non-anthropic universe. They will have to wait for many years to be measured and reach the gates of evolution. But as I emphasise, it is never too late to start.

Why? Because among the residents of the mortal realms, none are the same. We all come from different directions, and so we cannot all book a seat at the banquet. We are not equal in the process of evolution. We have each spent a different amount of time becoming evolved. And just as we do not come from the same direction, it is also true that we do not go in the same direction after.

My ambition is that we move forward after our departure from this planet. But it will not be together, because we are not at the same stage of evolution. We may move forward—or not backward—but it will not be hand in hand. We are not the same; not before, not now, nor after. Is that clear, dear friend?

Yet, the mortal realm of Earth is a meeting place for us all. It offers us the possibilities of training and education on our evolutionary way. The challenges here are at the highest degree of difficulty. I liken this planet to a prison, where convicts from all walks of life and people of various educational and spiritual levels are forced to coexist. What this entails is a dreadful and terrible situation where the animalistic instincts of lesser humans dominate socially and culturally, resulting in a living hell for the rest, as you saw in chapter 2. It is a formidable training ground indeed.

The cosmic role of the Earth, as decided by the Composers of the universe, is to welcome new converts, who are broad on the scale of diversity but are in the early stages of spiritual evolution. The importance of the Earth is as a school for beginners training in spiritual experiences. These are entities who before arriving on Earth lived in other realms of mortality similar to Earth but failed to evolve at least at one stage.

Backwards means everywhere in worse personal circumstances. This may be a planet equal to Earth in the early 21st century or earlier. Based on my model, there is no other planet in the mortal realms more technologically advanced than us. As Earthlings, we are very near to the top of our potential, and we know this because we have already moved quickly in the direction of self-destruction. Other species have fallen into self-destruction in this phase of civilisation too. Perhaps billions of others have already self-destructed and disappeared forever.

So, there are astronomically many rock planets like Earth that are friendly for the development of life and intelligent life. Yet, what separates them is not the material of the planet but the level of the current civilisation on each planet. There are many rock planets with various levels of current civilisation. Some are now as we were in Ancient Egypt, others as we were in Ancient Rome or Athens, and some as we were in the 1980s of Earth's civilisation, my favourite decade.

The myth of the ego

Why might we fail to evolve, you may wonder? One of the key reasons is the illusion of the ego. Yes, the ego is a myth. It does not exist. It is just another illusion, one that we have lived under for many years. In fact, it is one of the many terrifying illusions that humans are obliged to live under and praise, kept captive as spiritually inexperienced people. Anyone who dares to question the existence of the ego risks being scoffed at and facing attacks on their character. Nevertheless, let us degrade the ego and banish it into outer space.

Understand that the whole structure of this civilisation is based on beliefs such as the ego. The model of the ego, which those in the Dark Rooms impose upon you, means there will always be competition among the subjects of the global empire of money.

Notice the very important detail here. The Dark Rooms force the ego upon you to put you in constant conflict with everyone, but the tenants of the Dark Rooms are fully dissociated from the ego. That is, they operate on the basis that the ego applies to you, but not to them! So they choose to be invisible, without a specific identity. Their choice of invisibility is certainly wise. In no case do they need to enter into discussions and disputes with expendable humanity, who are merely tools for their usage.

So, you remain trapped in the net of the ego, competing and clashing with everyone except for your rulers. Competition between subjects always results in there being no prospect for an uprising of the multitude, since the individuals within the multitude are drawn into personal rivalries and passions that result from the struggle for dominance over one another's ego. This means that the masses will never overthrow the rulers.

The ego also works as a predator of your time. We have talked extensively about the rest of the predators of your time (such as sports, social media, and smartphones), and how you are unknowingly turned into prey. But do you notice how the ego is a predator of your time? In the context of the ego, there is a strong conviction that you are unique and so on a daily basis, you struggle to prove that you are superior to someone, to some people, or even to all people.

In my opinion, this is why social media has become so popular with uneducated people these days. In this medium, the people and the whole system, including so-called "stars", strive to emerge as singularities and eminent people through the posting of comments, photos, and videos. Everyone hunts manically for praise, likes, follows, and shares.

On social media, people speak with unbelievable ease about their private lives and personal details as if they are great events that everybody needs to know about! As if other humans will miss out on something by not knowing these details of their lives. Well, not only will other people *not* miss out on anything, but you are also wasting your own time. Sharing your life in this way does not give you the slightest value. The nature of consciousness is against you, and against the model of the ego.

Thus, the fact that virtually everyone will fail to evolve and essentially "leave as they came" is because they fail to break free from the patterns of illusions. They fail to avoid the idolatrous life imposed on them by the global system of power. They waste their time in this mortal realm without any progress, trapped by the predators of time—the ego included—set by those in the Dark Rooms. They are born as slaves of the system, and they leave as slaves of the system. They will miss the opportunity for evolution.

There are also those who raise the flag of doubt and display a rebellious attitude throughout their life, even abandoning the concept of the ego. Despite this, they often find that their success is limited to a personal level and they are exhausted by their lifelong doubt and a constant feeling that "something isn't right." Perhaps you have even felt this yourself. They know that things could be different, but they lack the necessary spiritual background to evolve.

Now, for first time ever, you have that opportunity because this book delivers the message and the five fundamental principles to start your evolution. Before now, no one ever evolved to reach the conscious realms. If you decide to leave your ego and start the procedure of learning and evolving, you will be at stage one. And since you are at stage one, you cannot go back to zero. You will be at stage one until you progress and evolve.

Look around you. Look at your pets; go outside and look at the birds, the animals, and the fish. What do you think of them? Hey, they are you in the past. More clearly, you were them in the past. That is level zero. When you have advanced from level zero to level one, it is impossible to return to level zero, although it is very possible that your beloved pets one day will advance to level one.

Of course, you may question why it is obligatory to be involved in this process rather than left alone to decide the end without an ever-after? Well, you have no such power to decide. You are not a member of the Society of Composers. You are not a resident of the conscious realms. You are not a Supreme Being. You are just a naive, uneducated boson of consciousness. So, who are you to decide the end without an ever-after? Wake up! You are not the owner, nor the engineer of consciousness. Your choice is to evolve or be stuck in the mortal realms forever.

The brain colonists

Of course, since I do not believe in the ego and do not join in the mania of social media, you may well wonder why you should listen to me? What authority do I have? Well, my strong belief in the existence of the non-anthropic universe arises through my constant communication with the Supreme Beings and the batches of powerful knowledge I receive on a daily basis through Einstein's wormhole method.

It emerged in my brain as a strong belief based on the undiscovered law of spontaneous appearance. It emerged from natural freedom in choice. It emerged spontaneously as powerful knowledge in my systematic application of the Fundamental Principles in my life and my constant study of the behaviour of nature.

My strong belief that the conscious realms are not bound by human laws was spontaneously created. Likewise my thesis that the conscious realms are governed by non-anthropic laws superior to the laws discovered in the material universe. My thesis came from the Supreme Beings.

. Indeed, we are all potential receivers of visitors from the conscious realms. We have an extra-terrestrial origin, since we all carry a consciousness that is not native to Earth. Therefore, some of us have constant neo-colonisations in our brains throughout our lives.

Personally, I have changed skin 12 times within the last 6 years, a concept that reflects the nature of some reptiles. This means that I have received many successive arrivals of Supreme Beings who have settled in my brain over the years. They bypassed the known paths by travelling through spiritual wormholes, and they found fertile chemical soil in my brain.

I felt every arrival of these colonists. I was completely neutral in emotion, but each arrival was accompanied by an internal, sweet relief. The arrivals always happen very early in the morning, just before dawn, and the former being gives its place to the new arrival. Some beings return to their homeland after their mission, while some travel to other mortal realms if people like me invite them. As there is no ego, their rotation is not emotional beyond a feeling of serenity and solidarity within the other beings. True solidarity as a species does not exist on Earth—only as an idea.

On their gracious and decisive excursions from the conscious realms, the Supreme Beings come here with a purpose. They come to settle in the brains of those who have the capacity to host them and invite them to come. They massively enhance our brain's capacities. They improve brain function and its powers astronomically. Thus, they help us to evolve when they are invited. Other humans on Earth may have the capacity to invite these beings but are not aware of it, and therefore are not aware of the existence of Supreme Beings.

You may be surprised to read about the arrival of colonists in the brain. After all, it is a concept that has never been explored before. Some will find it frightening, while others will reject it as being "crazy". If you find the idea frightening, I remind you of the nature of consciousness and the curious relationship of WE-I-ONE. Because of this relationship, we are both us and others at the same time. This is why the arrival of new colonists in the brain is completely peaceful and without any emotion.

There is nothing to fear, because when a colonist arrives, your daily life goes on as normal, smoothly and harmoniously. The new settler is a friend, companion, and effort-enhancer. Having a colonist does not mean that your individual self disappears. The being that is "you" is simply enhanced with a new dynamic, fresh ideas, and powerful knowledge from a higher level.

If you are concerned that there might be malicious entities who may colonize your brain, this is unequivocally not possible. There are no malicious beings with the ability to colonise us, as such beings are far below us on the evolutionary scale. Malicious beings are everywhere, and I am not talking about leprechauns or ghosts. I am talking about people. You can see them every day in the streets and squares. Malicious beings are just physical people who are deceived by illusions.

In other words, they are conscious humans who have formed demanding or destructive mindsets, leading them to become rapists, murderers, terrorists, or criminals. You may detest or loathe these people, but note that they have no capacity to disturb you spiritually. They may leave a bad taste in your mouth, but they are spiritually inferior so they cannot cause any damage to the spiritually superior.

You who has abandoned the myth of the ego are above such beasts. When we are tied to the ego, we cannot evolve. So here, let us abandon the ego forever. Thus, I do not ask you to follow me. I do not give a hoot whether you follow me or not. In fact, if you try to discover who I truly am, you will not find me, because I use a pen name. You may reach me via this book's website, as described earlier, but please allow me to live invisibly. Do not follow me, because I am not an ego-man, and my duty is simply to present the way to evolve.

Time for change

Yes, it is time to evolve, because otherwise you are trapped here in the mortal realms. Do you know that? There is a trap set up against you. You are doomed to age, decay, become ugly, and die. Nobody will care whether you were super rich in your huge mansion or a homeless, drunk man roaming the streets. You are doomed to be considered equal to the drunk man walking the streets if you fail to evolve. You will merely reappear in another mortal realm, worse off. So, now is the time to abandon your anthropic thinking, behaviours, and actions.

The anthropic principles are designed to fail. The pillars of the anthropic model are: the ego, structural thought in observing the behaviour of nature, physical determinism, reductionism, and the Big Bang Theory. From this failed model, we will keep the capacity for structural thinking—the amazing brain property gifted to us by the Egyptians and the Ionians—but we must reject all of the other pillars.

The structural thinking model enabled the Egyptians to achieve personal success against the odds and build the monumental pyramids and artworks we admire today. Structural thinking is a privilege for those who apply it in their lives, as it means that you are able to connect the boxes. Do you remember the maths fact-boxes from chapter 5? Where mathematicians fail to realise the existence of the infinite number of other boxes, so they think that by solving one box, they universally solve all of the problems and queries?

With the structural thinking method, you may solve the problem in the box while at the same time taking into account the parameters of the other unsolved boxes. So, now you know that you must connect the boxes, you must always consider all of the parameters before making any decision-solution.

By connecting the boxes, taking into account all of the probable parameters surrounding you, then you will have the opportunity to become a composer in your everyday life within the areas of your activities. Hey friend, dare to connect the boxes, dare to become a composer in your life—dare to make the difference!

Thus, we must retain the titanic brain property of structural thought, but we must reject the other pillars. You have seen how the myth of the ego produces greed and anomalies in human behaviour and social morals. These pillars worked very well until the early 21st century, but they no longer serve us, so we no longer need them. It is time for us to abandon them. *This era demands the new, the non-anthropic.*

So, I invite you to join the non-anthropic universe, the ego-free life, and the simple and natural way of living. Now that you understand the true nature of things, it is time to wake up! Forget the notion of the ego. Change the way you see the world, change your attitude, start thinking in a non-anthropic way. Rethink the world you live in, overcome this illusionary anthropic world, and become the light of the world.

PART 4

THE TROPHIES OF VICTORY

Chapter 9

THE FIVE TROPHIES

So far, you have discovered shocking and controversial concepts in this book. Now, we will proceed with equal boldness to consider important laws in the application of the Spontaneous Forces. As with the other concepts, these notions may lead to a violent conflict inside your mind, but please remember that such conflicts are essential for your improvement, and in the early stages of your spiritual evolution, they cause the effect of perception.

They are vital to gain the wonderful five trophies of:

1. Unified time
2. Collective observation
3. Bodily intelligence
4. Neutralisation
5. Freedom from the bonds of time and death

In this chapter, you will discover these trophies. Please note that they are not my discovery alone. Whatever any member of the species discovers, the discovery belongs to the whole of the species. I am not alive on my own; I live with you. I could not do or achieve anything alone. Even feats such as writing a book are not done alone.

1. The trophy of unified time

In the mortal realms, what we experience is time flowing uninterrupted at our expense. When it comes to this time, Earthlings treat everything in life as individual events. This is understandable, because time on Earth has strange properties—to the ordinary person, time appears to accelerate, especially as we age. If you leave it unchecked, then human time will crush you. The day will come when you will be a physical and spiritual mess, with no purpose whatsoever, and nothing to anticipate except for your impending death. This is the miserable story of spiritually uneducated people. However, when you enter the evolutionary way and begin to have spiritual experiences, you will become free from the bonds of time and death, as you will see in the next trophy.

As an individual who practises this secret New Fundamental Life, time gradually acquires a neutral direction, exactly as it does in the conscious realms—it becomes unified. Then, you can stop hunting after events. Instead, *you* create the events. In this way, you have the great privilege of overcoming time.

You know the properties and behaviours of anthropic time. You know that the anthrophic sense of time was born in the mind of the first human who appeared on Earth. You know that the universe has a much larger history than that of man. You also see that ordinary, uneducated people are victims of the anthropic nature of time, and it continues to flow at their expense. As a result, many people shudder at the nature of time and wonder what trap they are caught in. They tremble when it comes to the nature of moments—"Moments flee and nothing remains," they say.

By contrast, the notion of unified time frees you from the limitations faced by ordinary, uneducated people on Earth. In this notion of time, every moment you live only makes sense if it is connected to all of the previous moments and all of the subsequent moments. Otherwise, there is nothing but the huge illusion that you are living in the present separate from the past and the future, and therefore you are non-existent outside of each moment.

With the achievement of time unification, moments cease to make sense separately, like individual lightning bolts on a horizon that you will never see again. Through unification, the moment before your departure from this planet is linked to every preceding moment in your life as an integral whole.

Unified time frees you from the agony of the moments that come and go. Any separation between the past and the present is eliminated. Every moment is connected to all of the past and all of the future. It is a wave function of moments, an intellectual manoeuvre that enables us to become free from the shackles of time. All of your notions of "how fast time passes" disintegrate, as do some people's beliefs that after a certain age, time accelerates. With unified time, your human age even becomes irrelevant.

The way of freedom

Of course, unified time is my own invention. It is neither a revelation nor a new law; it is an invention. However, the current notion of time that humans follow is also an invention of the human mind. It came from a time when man was primitive and lived in forests and caves. Scientists have adopted this primitive invention, and to this day, they bicker over the properties of simple, primitive time.

By contrast, unified time solves many problems that have occupied people's minds. For example, in the context of unified time, there is no way that we can accept scientific theories as "proven" because we know they will be overthrown in the future with new data and new observations. In fact, we cannot accept anything as permanent, as it is no more than a temporary thing until it is replaced by the next thing.

Understanding and applying the concept of unified time in your daily life also works as a constant exercise of the brain and way to engage with life. You may begin to become romantic, engaging in poetry and the arts, and being mystical. You will become one with the garden of your home, which due to your new conception of time will be transformed into a garden of the whole world.

You will meet people on the street, in your workplace, at social gatherings, and feel that you are not like them! You will feel that you are something much higher than them, but this feeling has no selfish, arrogant background. It will be a genuine and above all *spontaneous* feeling of spiritual superiority because you are free from the shackles of time, while they are not.

On the last day of your life, you are eternally free, as all of the fleeting moments of your life join together collectively. For this to occur, an active brain is required until the last second of your presence in this mortal realm, but have no fear—you have the chance to prepare by starting to consolidate your mind now.

I remind you of the requirement for patience when understanding this notion. It is not easy to understand new concepts. In this case, you must disregard the split model of the past-present-future that is primitive time. In the new context of unified time, it is possible to see life from an entirely different viewpoint, one that proudly takes you along new paths of understanding.

2. The trophy of collective observation

This is the pair trophy of unified time. It is another trophy that can be used to great effect in our daily movements, as we understand through the notion of collective observation and unification that each movement links to our other movements.

We must not endanger our physical integrity, nor allow ourselves to be attacked by chance. Have you noticed how often people are injured in their homes? They fall down stairs, slip on the ground, fall in the bathroom, hit their heads on furniture and walls, tread and sit on objects they failed to notice, climb a ladder and crash to the ground.

Then there are the countless daily accidents outside the home, on the streets, in the squares, in the parks, in the workplace, in the car while driving—all due to absent-mindedness, carelessness, and a lack of self-discipline and concentration. It is why people lose their personal belongings, keys, telephones, money, sunglasses and eyeglasses, bags, and ID.

The reason why this occurs is because people do not realise the notion of unified time and collective observation. Collective observation means that anything perceived as the result of an observation or an experiment must be linked to the whole of known knowledge. Moreover, possible logical inconsistencies and arbitrary interpretations should be ruled out before coming to the final conclusion about any one thing.

For example, the Big Bang Theory, the claimed discovery of gravitational waves, photographs of black holes, cosmic inflation theory, Microwave Background radiation, and so on. All of these examples lack collective observation, and I reject all of them as unproved, primitive models or events that belong to science fiction and not science fact.

Without such collective observation in their lives, humans are the epitome of chance, and so they enter a constellation of suffering. They end up in hospital injured or suffer fractures, financial losses, or wastes of their time. Thus, the most important applications of unified time and collective observation are the caution and self-discipline that we must invest in every second of our lives. With this winning mentality, we do not allow chance to invade the field of our personal activity.

The way of time management

Now that you recognise the constant agreement of all things in the flow of unified time and collective observation, you are privileged in your social environment. Your fellow Earthlings do not recognise these things. Thus, all of your actions have a framework of continuity, where your moments agree with all the previous and upcoming ones. Your own definition of events is an agreement between events within the given space-time of the current mortal realm of Earth.

Here, the very important issue of time management arises. Time management means that you choose when to participate and when to withdraw. Think about how many useless things happen in your daily life as an Earthling. How much nonsense, how much vanity, how much incoherence happens to everyone. Meetings, conferences, social gatherings, social media, and the sharing of useless information. For most people, all moments are lost, forgotten, or deleted, and contribute nothing but hypocrisy or boredom.

By contrast, with the higher knowledge of unified time and collective observation, you weaken all of those things. You choose which moments you will strengthen and which you will weaken from their burden. Your decision to participate in any event means new, useful experiences, peace, and harmony because when you choose to participate, you have an understanding of the value of moments.

A simple example of this can be observed when watching somebody deliver a speech. The "audience" is full of people asleep in their seats or immersed in their smartphones. Even those who watch do not remember a word of these speeches! The reason why is a lack of value in the moments of their lives. Everything weighs on them.

As an implementer of unified time, do not participate in such gatherings if you judge that they do not offer you anything. I do not. On the contrary, I participate with enthusiasm and passion wherever I have something to offer as a speaker, or I participate as a listener with polite behaviour and a caring smile. The value of time management is an understanding of things that are worth your time and things that are not, whether they relate to your physical, mental, or spiritual health.

3. The trophy of bodily intelligence

With the trophy of unified time, it becomes a way of life and action. In understanding physical health in the context of unified time, you may become the master of bodily intelligence. Perhaps you are surprised to read about the "body's intelligence". However, it is important to realise that in the life you lived before now, your standards, attitudes, and ideals were insufficient, including the model of nutrition you followed. None of these helped you in the evolutionary process. Perhaps you made no progress and were stagnant, and spiritually, you were a cabbage. Yes, you were a spiritual cabbage.

Just as there is intelligence in your brain, through which you build thoughts, so there is intelligence in animals, trees, and every form of life, including your own body. This is what I call the "intelligence of known matter", which is absolutely different from the intelligence of evolved matter and intelligent particles, as this type of intelligence only appears in the conscious realms.

If you want to become the ruler and master of your body and utilise your body's intelligence as atrophy, then you must understand that your body reacts aggressively towards you when it is suffering. Bodily intelligence covers all aspects of our body, but let us consider diet as an example, since it is one of my favourite topics.

On a daily basis, you must be careful about what you eat and the quantity of food you consume because your attitude towards your plate now is related to the physical health of your body at any time. If your behaviour now is wise, then you may prevent many violent reactions in your body later. You must realise that everything is connected, as explained in the notion of unified time, and so all of your eating behaviours are part of the chain of your moments.

Unfortunately, as I explained earlier, Earthlings treat everything as individual events. Thus, they believe that destructive eating behaviours in this moment will have no effect on their body in all of the other moments. It never crosses their mind that they may, at some point, find themselves in a hospital bed because of their greedy, foolish, and naive consumption habits. And so they end up exiting life under the terrible punishment and suffering of diseases that stem from eating unhealthy food in many or all of their moments.

So, when you are choosing what to consume, think collectively about all of the moments that will be affected by this choice in this moment. Remind yourself that the moment does not exist today, cut off from yesterday and tomorrow. Everything flows in constant communication between your moments.

If you think I am being harsh, it is no secret that a poor diet has terrible effects on the human body. One study found that almost half of human deaths were directly linked to poor diet, leading to illnesses such as stroke, type 2 diabetes, and heart disease.[31] Note that these deaths were not only due to consuming unhealthy products such as processed food, sugars, and salt, but also a lack of consuming healthy items such as fruit, vegetables, nuts, seeds, and grains.

Maintaining a healthy diet is not difficult, though so many inaccurate things are written about food and cooking methods by so-called "experts" and laymen. So let us look at the reality of food and cooking in a practical application.

The harmonic ritual of cooking

First, it is important to understand that almost all fresh vegetables can be eaten raw, but this in no way dictates that we must or should consume them raw. We are not herbivorous animals that eat raw grasses and leaves found in nature. We choose to eat many plants cooked. Cooking food is a gift, a talent. It is communication with nature and the items that our Earth produces.

I am fortunate to have the best cook in the world at my home, Joti, who I mentioned earlier. Joti has unbelievable talents in communicating with nature. She cooks for me daily and creates an unparalleled atmosphere with the love, kindness, and care she puts into the cooking process.

The start of Joti's cooking ritual is the washing. She knows best how to wash and purify the Earth's products. Then, she cooks them with remarkable geometry, paying close attention to the finer details, demonstrating her love and respect for me and those she is cooking for.

She is the master of nature and fire. She knows exactly when vegetables are ready to leave the fire to be served, not a second early, not a second late. She garnishes her cooking with fresh lemon and olive oil. She finds the perfect harmony of the Goldilocks zone, the ideal conditions to maximise the nutritional yield of vegetables, spices, and products of nature under her culinary responsibility.

As Joti is from India, she uses miraculous spices from India and Asia in her cooking, and I can no longer go without these spices. Maybe I have become addicted. Yet, it is an addiction that only causes me beneficial effects, and the right thing is to have a good addiction in our lives. The three miraculous spices I am addicted to and eat in every meal are turmeric, ginger, and black pepper.

Joti also uses garlic in a wonderful way, teaching me that it is better to eat garlic raw. When she does cook garlic, it is in hot water for no longer than two minutes. Fresh and almost raw, it is peeled, cut into small pieces, then mixed with yoghurt and a few drops of honey. I eat it and feel like Cyclops!

Throughout the cooking process, Joti faithfully follows the doctrine of harmony. She offers her own energy to the process, which I call bio-electric energy, to the extent that I feel like a Supreme Being on Earth during my eating ritual. Yes, it is a ritual! I enjoy nature's offspring in wonderment, enriched with love and bio-electric energy. I absorb the maximum potential of the nutritional load, since Joti finds the Goldilocks zone with geometric mastery and precision to create the perfect dishes.

A lack of harmony in cooking

By contrast, let us look at what occurs in most restaurants, cafes, and places of mass catering. The only thing such venues care about is snatching money from your wallet. They consider you, the customer, an upright victim! There is no love, no ritual, in their cooking. They may sell you sophisticated combinations of ingredients and complex flavours that have no use for your body's intelligence. But their poor-quality foods will more likely contribute to your hospital admissions, and even to the cemetery!

Consider the meat, poultry, and fish sold in restaurants—where do they come from? From manufactured farms, obviously. If a restaurant claims that it offers quality and authenticity, then it should show you where its meat, fish, and poultry are procured. Otherwise, do not go in. Do not pay for your premature death!

Personally, I do not buy such foods. I eat food that is very simple, plain, and natural. I am fortunate to live on an island where I can find small, independent producers of eggs, cheese, yoghurt, non-farmed poultry, non-farmed fresh fish from the seas, and vegetables. I never eat red meat, processed meats, or products related to red meat. From personal experience, I do not believe that red meat is friendly to the human digestive system. On the contrary, it is hostile.

I reject the ideology of the mainstream establishment that "red meat is good for you". The global food trade cannot exist without red meat and all of its by-products. That is why scientists and "experts" ensure you are aware of the "benefits" of red meat in your diet, and the precious chemical properties of meat that they claim make it an indispensable, integral part of every human's diet.

I am outraged by their irresponsibility, and I invite you to ignore them. Their motivations stem from their funding, which comes from the colossal companies in the meat industry. However, I am not a vegetarian ideologist either. I reject all ideologies. I do not care what vegetarians do. I simply write about events that I have identified with my first-hand experiences.

Let us not even discuss smoking. Would you abuse your body in such a way? Remember the unification of moments mean that each cigarette consumed affects every other moment. Do you drown your liver in alcohol? Personally, I stay far away from alcohol, but I ask you to consider your own body and unified time. If you only consume moderate amounts of alcohol and you eat a friendly, healthy diet, then it is possible to look after your body and be a candidate for the new evolutionary race. You must look after your body so that it is your ally and not your enemy.

Of course, we may look after our nutrition and consumption to maintain our health, but this does not account for genetic and hereditary issues, which we cannot control. We can only look after our daily diet and activity levels. For example, in the case of diabetes, people must measure their blood glucose levels and maintain the correct balance.

Understand that our body and mind are the vessels that must carry us through to our exit from this mortal realm. Thus, we should strengthen our immune system to the fullest extent, as it is our body's first and main line of defence against potential invasions. Look after the vessel that must carry you through this life.

4. The trophy of neutralisation

When you understand your body and mind through the principle of self-confidence, and you observe your daily movements, you can achieve the greatest application of collective observation and unified time—neutralisation. Neutralisation is the mutual extermination of emotional burdens, and it is a collective attitude towards life and action. However, it is not nirvana.

A mystic may touch the peak that is neutralisation by increasingly applying and experiencing unified time in their daily life using their new perception. In this attitude towards life, your emotions begin to converge. Inevitably, gradually, and lawfully, they will coincide completely. Through practice, both joy and sadness will be mitigated so much that the mystic will experience complete neutralisation, the mutual extermination of emotional burdens.

Nothing brings joy to the mystic of eternity, and nothing causes sorrow. No emotion touches the mystic. No event causes the slightest interest to the mystic, only the everlasting peace and tranquillity of harmony, the meditation of the conscious realms, and the path to eternal evolution. All of the emotional burdens imposed and spread by the current failed system of government are nullified.

However, the neutralisation of joy, happiness, sadness, stress, sorrow, and misery does not mean an exodus from this world. Under no circumstance does neutralisation mean a lack of motivation to live and act. On the contrary, it means an enormous motivation to set the order, decide the rules, and deliver the fairness lacking in the world. This lack of fairness occurs because of the monumental greediness of the species, and it is the main reason why this planet suffers so heavily and is becoming increasingly unfriendly and inhospitable to the development of life and intelligent life.

Thus, neutralisation strengthens the capacities for anger, outrage, and revenge—together with the huge motivation to set the rules and mercilessly punish the enemies of life on Earth. You see, mystics know that the world is one of violence, and that the universe is one of constant violent and explosive processes. For the mystic, no one will go unpunished for any form of violence against the world. The mystic is against needless violence, but at the same time, neutralisation is the rock on which any forms of violence against the Earth will be crushed.

Even if only one living being achieves the trophy of neutralisation, this is enough to decide the necessary structural changes for fairness on this planet (which the unknown Jesus strived to achieve). The mystic holds the trophy, but the whole species will cheer because they will benefit from the results of the mystic's epic battles against those in the Dark Rooms who rule the current phase of civilisation on this planet. Friend, never be surprised. Even one achiever is enough, but more than one is welcome and will only boost the forces acting against those in the Dark Rooms.

As you can see, neutralisation is the majestic annihilation of emotional burden, but the mystic does not commit suicide, does not turn into a hermit, and does not withdraw from the world. The mystic knows their natural origin, which is the origin of the universe. They know that like the universe, they were born spontaneously everywhere but not somewhere (remember that there are no space-time points before the genesis of the material universe) and they expand elsewhere and forever, which in the conscious course means evolving forever until they are reborn.

They know that the Spontaneous Forces are the dominant form of power and law in the universe, and that they can become a shareholder and member of these forces. They do not fear their inevitable mortal death, because they know that this death does not mean eternal death.

5. The trophy of freedom from the bonds of time and death

Human beings untrained in spiritual education will inevitably seem like brittle, yellowing autumn leaves that may be snatched away by the wind and carried off at any moment. They are victims of chance, and their lives are unfair battles against time and death. Sadly, the vast majority of humans fail to even realise that they will lose.

Understanding the concept of unified time is a requirement to break free from the shackles of Earth. However, the full maturation of this understanding will come to your mind only a few moments before your biological end. In the context of unified time, your departure—death—not only causes no fear but is in fact the sweetest of all experiences. For the mystic, who is spiritually educated, they understand the value of life, but more importantly, that death is not something to be feared.

In that beautiful, long-awaited moment, everything about the human species and the planet Earth will collapse as non-existent and useless. Time will work in a neutral direction, moving neither forward nor backward. At that moment, you—the mystic—will know that all of the moments of the human past are united as conscious experiences in the next stage after the Earth, the conscious realms. You will be leaving your mortal self, having successfully completed your Earthly mission to evolve.

However, you must accept the possibility that from the vast number of mortal realms, only one species successfully moves to the conscious realms. Of the billions of ordinary species across billions of mortal realms, a whole species may be marionettes, and only one may progress to the conscious realms.

This might sound shocking to you, as it is very different from what we are taught by traditional religions in their top-down learning method. It is a requirement for evolution to understand shocking new and powerful knowledge. Likewise, freedom from the bonds of death is different from the traditional teachings of religion, which believe it is achieved in heaven.

Though I am not against any religion, as I explained earlier, I do not accept any religious authority. I respect them all, and I reject them all. I believe that liberation cannot be achieved in commercial terms like "give to get". Thus, giving up something here on Earth will not deliver a reward in the conscious realms or the heavens as an exchange. The conscious realms do not operate based on Earthly attitudes and practices.

Join to previous paragraph instead of this one. Eternal death means zero, nothing, nonsense. From time to time, I hear ordinary people say that "humanity is cursed". It is not a matter of a curse. Something simpler is happening to you, dear friend. Stage one is your current phase of the evolvement process, and it is your unavoidable fate. There is no chance for you to escape this process through the death of your physical body or by believing that the death of your physical body will deliver you "back" to the un-worrying think-less freedom of non-existence. You cannot decide what will happen to you after the death of your miserable physical body. You are just a boson of consciousness, not consciousness as a whole.

With this understanding of the true nature of death, you may create value in every moment of your life. All of your current moments become important because they are an integral part of the conscious continuum. All of your present moments in any "now" acquire worth. They cease to be individual lightning bolts on the horizon of events that no one will remember, not even you. They will all refer to and lead to the point of unification, which is the last moment of your life on the planet. The Earthly illusion that others "live" but you will cease to does not concern you or affect you.

Understanding the value of moments is a huge spiritual conquest. You are now privileged compared to other Earthlings because all of your moments exist and have value in relation to the point of unification. Now, you can freely study everything because you know that it has value. You may escape the power that keeps you tied to Earth's time. You are like a spaceship liberated from Earth—with the opportunity to travel through moments of enjoyment in the vast space of the conscious experience.

Bearing all of this in mind, it is time to throw your old ideas of time into the grave as quickly as possible—though you now know that time, quickness, and graves are not what you once thought. Unified time has freed you from the human concerns about decay, death, and fear of the unknown.

The trophy cabinet

As a participant in the New Fundamental Life, the perception and application of unified time and collective observation are your trophies. As a result, you are almost equipped to create the past, to be a shareholder of the Spontaneous Forces through communication with the conscious realms, to activate your structural thought, to connect the boxes, to be the winner of the revolutionary intelligence race, to evolve forever, and never look back again...

However, the trophy cabinet of the conscious realms' entry criteria needs one extra thing. What else do you need in the cabinet? Patience, obviously. There is no need to rush things—whatever will come will come. One day, you will be evolved in the areas of intelligence and consciousness, separated from the current version of the human species.

Of course, it is not easy to abandon your lifestyle from one day to the next to enter the New Fundamental Life. It was not easy for me either. My personal battles lasted for many decades. Patience is the reason why I am ahead of you in the evolutionary process. Yet, you can achieve these trophies, and this is why I advise you to always maintain the best relationship with patience.

Also understand that you are not alone. Myriads are at the same stage as you are now, in the early era of spiritual development and evolution. Not only on this planet, but on countless other mortal planets, so you are definitely not alone. Just look up at the night sky. Look at the light from the stars, and think how many of those stars are alive now, how many have solar planet systems, how many have been born whose light we are yet to receive, and how many are material universes...

With this realisation, do you see that is impossible to be alone on your journey of evolution?

Chapter 10

THE CREATION OF THE PAST

Welcome to the final chapter of this book. By now, you know about the world you live in and about the universe and its unseen parts. You know what you need to do to break the shackles of this planet and this mortal life. However, to break free, you need to have the spontaneous self-confidence of being to create a past worthy of escaping. This capacity is active in all areas of human activity. So, in this chapter, we will examine some practical applications of creating the past.

Understanding the notion of the past

Lack of fear of death is not the only benefit of unified time. Due to the unbreakable nature of unified time, the notion of the past is instantly detached from what the average man or woman considers it to be. To you, the past now means not that which *has* happened, but that which *is* happening. By creating the past, you avoid the trap of time-quicksand. You create the events, and the events never create you. In this way, the ability to create your past becomes an invaluable trophy.

Understand in your creation of events that efforts are plentiful and goals are many. It is impossible for anyone to achieve all of their personal goals. There are no people in this mortal realm who can achieve that. But if you try with all your might, with all of your energy and enthusiasm, ignoring the denials you get from your surroundings, then you might accomplish the ultimate goal of knocking on the door to the conscious realms. When you achieve one of your goal, you knock on the door. By knocking the door, you announce to them "Hey, I am here, and I am evolving".

THE TEMPLE OF CONSCIOUSNESS

Know that if you even reach the door, then you have succeeded—even if you have only achieved a few of your personal goals! It simply does not matter. If you have arrived at the door and knocked on it, you are already successful. Opening the door is equivalent to recording the past. The door must open at least one time to become a fact.

Not opening it means you did everything you could, but the door did not open. The past was not created. But the fact that it did not open does not bother you at all. You simply keep trying.

Only the past can be created and not the future. You cannot put goals into a starting point and push them into the future, do you understand? Very few of the goals you set now will reach the door, and even fewer will be recorded as the definitive past. And since you cannot know in advance which goals within an overall goal will be fulfilled, then you have no chance of creating the future. Simply put, you do not have a cause to create a cause and an effect, and you cannot cancel the natural law of cause and effect. In short, you cannot know in advance which goals you will achieve, so you can never create the future, only the past.

When you do accomplish goals, you record them as the past. Of course, they are also recorded by those in the conscious realms, the Supreme Beings who follow and record everything you do. When your great moment of encountering the Supreme Beings arrives, they will analyse your past. All of the unfulfilled goals will be deleted and not recorded anywhere because they did not contribute to the creation of the past. Stories of unfulfilled goals ultimately do not have any effect, and so they will be eliminated because they contribute nothing to the past.

The achievement of small feats

Us educated mystics have a holistic attitude toward life, and this allows us to create our own past. To do this for yourself, you must complete both small and large feats. The small feats are personal goals—for example, delivering a public talk that excites the audience and will remain eternally engraved in their memory.

For example, a small feat that I once accomplished was gaining victory over a banking giant in court without a lawyer. Yes, this really happened! I captured the minds of both the judges and the bank's lawyers during a trial that lasted four years. My lawyers were the Spontaneous Forces, which acted invisibly and quietly, such that no one could escape the outcome I demanded. They were obliged to surrender to my terms without realising the powers activated against them. It was the most amazing small feat I have ever accomplished.

Importantly, we must *not* consider the factor of time in achieving small and large feats. Doing so takes time, and spontaneous revelations may happen very slowly, being that they are on another level of space-time. As a beginner, you ought not to have high expectations. You will achieve such feats and revelations with patience, meditation, abstinence from idolatrous habits, and more patience—regardless of the time and limitations of your physical body.

The law of alternative paths

To achieve these feats, you must understand the law of alternative paths, which takes two forms. The primitive form applies to ordinary members of the species with the governor of randomness—and the advanced form, which applies to mystics only.

This law is exciting, even in its primitive form. I discovered it long ago when I realised that I was following one specific path of events but absolutely under the rules of randomness. This meant that I could have followed a different path of events if the randomness had created different dimensions. So I was following one path but at the same time, I was a candidate to follow many other paths.

Imagine someone driving a car. All of a sudden, they receive an emergency call. As a result, they change their scheduled route, and after a few minutes, a lorry crashes into them and they spend six months in hospital. Or say you plan to go to a specific restaurant but your friend suggests that you instead go to a new, very beautiful restaurant, so you change your mind and in the new restaurant you meet a lovely waitress, fall in love with her, and spend your whole life with her.

This notion was explored in a film called *Sliding Doors*, where a woman misses her train and the timeline splits into two, showing the alternate paths her life could have taken if she caught the train and if she did not. But unlike this film, my friend, the paths are oceanic in number. Truly, I could write thousands of them. Every day, the law of alternative paths applies to your life, to everybody's life. Imagine the process of buying a new car or a new house, imagine the thousands of histories of alternative paths that emerge because you have chosen this specific car or this specific house.

Okay, take a breath now, because I have just described to you the misery of being trapped in the nets of randomness. Thankfully, there is an advanced form of the law of alternative paths open to mystics. In the advanced form, there is no place for randomness. I hear ordinary people blaming bad luck for anything unfortunate that happens in their lives. For the mystic, there is no place for luck. The mystic governs their luck and creates positive results as per their desire. The mystic transforms the mythological "goddesses" of luck and randomness into power in their hands.

As an example of the advanced form in action, I decided to write and publish this book. It is one thing to publish a book, and it is another thing to sell that book. Do you understand this proposition? After seeing the measly number of copies sold, ordinary authors blame their bad luck. If their book happens to sell many copies, it is due to randomness. Well, I am not willing to leave the fate and destiny of my book to the mercy of randomness. I am the only person who will decide the selling path for my book.

The mystic does not count on others to decide the path for them. They decide their fate and destiny by activating the Spontaneous Forces, which is the second form of the law of alternate paths. In this method, the mystic, when faced with any situation, should anticipate the possible alternate paths ahead of them and the potential results they will receive. Then, they must use the power of "active seeking" to activate the Spontaneous Forces in their favour. Actively seeking the desired result means that the mystic will turn the sky upside down in order to activate the Spontaneous Forces.

For example, my duty is to exclude the paths that will prevent the commercial success of my book by calling on the Spontaneous Forces. Between my desire to sell and the actual selling point, I use "active seeking" to activate the Spontaneous Forces in my favour. In this case, it means actively researching marketing options. It is the opposite of sitting back and doing nothing yet expecting the universe to magically give you the answers.

When the mystic actively seeks the path, the Spontaneous Forces indicate which paths are doomed and shine a light on the paths that will lead to some form of success. In this manner, the mystic avoids the paths that will lead to certain failure.

Of course, we cannot know exactly what will happen in this mortal realm, and so the exact outcome of any path is an exciting mystery to behold. The law of alternate paths means that in the process of realising the path, many unexpected things will occur. For one thing, you will be lost and for another thing, you will be found! The surprises will succeed one another. Eventually, the path you emerge on may be different to the one you earlier aimed for.

Imagine you are a chef striving to create an original dish to impress people in its innovation, appearance, and taste. You imagine the alternative paths of your creations, actively seek the answers, and choose a potentially successful path to follow. On that path, you will constantly discover new mixes of materials until the final effect—the resulting plate—appears. It will relate in at least some way to what you originally imagined, but it will not be exactly as you envisioned because of the law of alternative paths. The same holds true for any kind of mystic, be it a painter, a composer of music, a theatre or film director, a poet, or a writer.

In my case, I chose the path to write this book, and I envisioned what this book would be. But during the course of writing, I captured thousands of new concepts that I did not know existed before embarking on this wonderful journey to Ithaca! I made unbelievable intellectual gains on the journey of writing. I enjoyed many spiritual moments of creative peace and experienced revelations from the conscious realms. When the book is released, the arrival in Ithaca will be equivalent to a pause in the revelation of new perceptions. However, the journey to the new Ithaca will begin soon after, because I am wise enough now to know what Ithaca means, as Cavafy says.

Similarly, when choosing how to market the book, from all of the alternative paths of potential success, I select very few for my book but I cannot know the exact outcome. With spontaneous self-confidence and the Spontaneous Forces highlighting the successful paths, I can avoid the certain paths to failure. This will nullify the mainstream beliefs that a first-time unknown author (as is my case) has zero chances of selling their book.

Some mainstream mugs claim that all first-time independent authors are doomed to sell between 0 and 100 copies, and if an author leaves the success of their book to fate, then that is a strong possibility. However, the Spontaneous Forces mean I will smash this estimate as a tennis player smashes the ball at the opposite side of the court. I will make the unthinkable thinkable.

By cancelling the "forces" of randomness and luck, you are the hero, the owner, the composer, and the engineer. You are a shareholder in the Spontaneous Forces and you command them to create your desired result, which means that you create your own past as the mystic.

However, understand that not counting on others to decide the path for you does not mean doing all of the work yourself. Of course, no one can be everywhere, doing everything. For example, I chose the independent path of writing this book. I chose the editor who I rated as a match for this book, and the cover designer, and so on. But for myself, I kept the duty of the head of marketing department. I am the composer of this book, with the people I have chosen to work alongside me.

If I had followed the mainstream path of publishing, who the hell would be my editor? I would not get to choose them, nor the cover of my book, nor anything else. What publisher knows my personality, my genes, my tactics, and my targets? If you trust any other person to choose the path for you, not only in selling a book but in life, then you are a loser by my definition. The mystic never lets somebody choose the path for them—the mystic chooses their own path from the potential successful paths, where unknown but wonderful results will emerge.

The path of one

When it comes to subjects such as alternative paths, humans often ask the questions, "Why am I me and not someone else? Why am I living now and not in the past? Why am I here and not elsewhere?"

Maths cannot help us here, because the answer always ends up within the boxes we place them. Nobody can answer why this is the case. Yet at least one person—your author—has realised that we are each following a path of events simultaneously. We are simply reacting to a path that is our own boson of consciousness, and so our own path is simply our experiences.

The others next to us, the potential others everywhere in the universe, and the others who have not yet been born—they are living our alternative course of events. This means an infinite number of paths and eternal life, regardless of our biological end.

This biological end, the death of the physical body, is by no means a sad event. At my father's funeral, I addressed the audience and gave them the message that me and my family did not carry any feeling of sadness, and that the audience would someday follow my father in abandoning their physical bodies. You are here now, but soon you will not be here, so where is the place for sadness?

In the mortal realms, nothing is more than soon. Both 10 years and 10 million years are "soon". Our biological end is just an expected event. If you give this event any importance, it is because you are trapped in the illusion of considering your current life as one unconnected to others. You are governed by randomness, an autumn leaf blown around the street by winds of randomness.

Yet, we are not one unconnected to others. We were the others in the past, we are the others of the future, and we are all of those who live in the current phase of the mortal realm here, elsewhere, and everywhere. We are parts of the Supreme Beings, parts of the Composers. We follow one path of events as bosons of consciousness, but as I have explained, we are not the whole.

We are the present, the past, and the future, at once and forever. We continue to carry our "unique existence", do not worry! We will still be judged as unique bosons by the Supreme Beings based on our choices of the path we follow. The path of the winner, not the loser, is the path to the evolutionary way.

Thus, we may choose our path, choose our past, and never leave randomness to decide for us. We may become the winners if we decide our fate, if we trust ourselves, and if we do not count on anyone to do the work for us, removing from our selected path the notion of being a loser. Thus, we may create the past of a winner.

Violently creating the past

There are multiple ways of creating your past, the first being a violent exploitation of events. Suppose you are the parent of a 2-year-old toddler and you like tennis, so you think, *"Ah, I'll create a tennis player"*. Thus, you set about creating the past of your young child.

First, you decorate the room where your child sleeps or spends most of their waking hours. You put up posters of tennis champions in characteristic poses during their moments of greatness. You place tennis balls and rackets around the home and garden. The atmosphere of tennis will be cultivated in your child's mind at the critical age of 18 months to 3 years old. This is the first period of "harvest" for a child's mind. This first harvest of images and impressions is critical in a child's future.

Second, you ensure that your child becomes familiar with the sport. You regularly put tennis matches on TV so they can watch it. Not just any matches, but the ones the champions participate in. This way, your child chooses one of the great champions through natural selection and begins to dream that one day, they will be like this star.

At the age of 4, with knowledge of the sport and one of the great champions in their mind's quiver, your child enters the courts. They begin learning the secrets of the sport from a capable and talented instructor. Their training is achieved by entering the child into a tennis academy. Here, they must learn the details concerning matches. Details are often the most important points in life.

Simultaneously, the child gains a spiritual mentor. The ideal mentor is a parent, as no one can better and more effectively build a child's spiritual personality than their parent. However, if the parents do not have the self-confidence to undertake this important task, then they choose the next-best mentor after themselves.

The next step is building your child's spiritual personality. In the context of spiritual practice, the mentor must teach the child discipline, the mental focus to achieve goals, and the unwavering, unyielding process of progress towards the top. Through their spiritual personality, they will learn to not tolerate weakness and know that defeat is necessary to bring out your weaknesses.

During their many years of study at the academy, the child will gradually begin to develop their unique abilities and talents through participating in training and tournaments. At some point, around the age of 18, a new tennis giant may emerge who will leave humanity speechless.

After the age of 18, their spiritual training is even more important, and it continues intensively at the same time as their physical education. As a result, the mentor will need to tighten the leash. They have to provide a solid ground for the champion candidate, making them comprehend the value of the life of an athlete away from partying, alcohol, smoking, and sex.

The young athlete must also appreciate and demonstrate the values of humility, kindness, and grit in the face of any circumstances. The mentor has to build a spiritual giant made of steel, but at the same time a noble person who is a shining example for the whole of society.

In this way, you can see how parents can violently create a tennis star's past.

Indeed, it is often the case that the past you create in life may be chosen by your parents, rather than by you. Parents regularly decide what their children will become by enrolling them in classes that interest them and pushing them towards sports or exploits they love. Be it ballet, football, the cello, or anything else.

This example is indicative of the path that many parents push their children down in various areas. Personally, I would never choose such tactics as they violate physical freedom and evolution by natural selection—and therefore violate all of the fundamental principles that I teach. While violent conflicts are necessary during the primitive stages of evolution, as happened in the history of the material universe, it should be up to each individual which past they create—and not the choice of their parents, teachers, or mentors.

[175]

The creation of a tennis star is a classic case of human trafficking. In other words, capturing a human brain in order for the parents to gain the benefits. It is forcing a person to become a slave of exploitation, and I say "slave" because this person will never know what their true mission on Earth is. Essentially, the end of their life will come and the only thing they will have "achieved" is premature fame and glory—and the money, illusions, and material "trophies" of our pagan age.

A new perception and perspective always emerges in a world that has nothing to be proud of. That time is now. We are moving away at the speed of light from big and small devils, such as ordinary people, malicious people, and those in the Dark Rooms, banking systems, politicians, the media, pornography, unhealthy food, smoking, and so on. We must go forth strongly and with enthusiasm. We must touch upon something that no Homo sapien has touched. We must dive into the heavenly depths of the ocean with full exploration equipment and spontaneous self-confidence.

Lovingly creating the past

Thankfully, there is another option to create your child's past. You can *positively* create the past for your children, making them candidates for evolution rather than imaginary tennis star candidates. If you are wondering why you should pursue this path, it is because as parents, you are responsible for lovingly, gently creating your child's past.

Until now, you most likely did not imagine that how you live and what you know is only current. You did not know the concept of unified time. Of course, because nobody in your life ever explained the concept of unified time. But now, as a shareholder of unified time, you have the duty to teach your children about it, and show them how to practice the New Fundamental Life.

On the opposite extreme of the tennis star parents, other parents may say "It's my child's life; I let them do what they want." Despite this assertion, they may follow their religion's rules of trafficking their children into the church to become the next obedient followers of the church's bullshit. They may allow the church to expand its power by offering donations or tithing. They may allow religion to dictate their child's choices and actions in life.

Or if they are not religious, they may leave their children unprotected in the chaotic world of smartphones, social media, and pornography. They may pay no attention to what their child is watching on the television or internet, only to express surprise when their child becomes violent or aggressive or makes nothing useful of their life.

Hey parents, it is time for you to become the composer of your child's life. As a composer, you must start with the right elements to create the new fundamental past for your child.

Who they are

Your children must first understand who they are; so teach your children who they are and importantly, who the others are. *Without decoration.* They must understand that titles, either in education or job titles, never contribute to true self-development and expansion. Whatever titles they have, these are just decorations. Teach your children that nationalities, names, religions, and social customs imposed on them by others are just another form of useless decoration. Brain capacities are not developed by decoration.

When they are old enough to understand this concept, teach your children to consider themselves naked in the morning, without titles, clothes, suits, uniforms, models, or any kind of decoration. They should always remember how weak, dirty, and vulnerable they are as human beings. Vulnerable to all kinds of diseases, accidents, violence and crime, natural wild phenomena, pain, and death. As humans, we are just dirty, weak, vulnerable, scared animals.

Teach your children that nobody is superior to them, and that nobody should suppress them. They should not be trampled underfoot, used as anybody's tool, or manipulated or controlled by others. This is an extremely important belief that you must build in your child's mind, inputting your highest effort and patience. The purpose of this is the development of self-awareness and spontaneous self-confidence of being for your children.

Consciousness vs. conscious-less

Your child must not only understand themselves, but also the nature of their surroundings.

Teach your children to see nature, animals, birds, fish, trees, seas, oceans, mountains, lakes, rivers, clouds, rains, and snow. Ensure that they recognise humankind as a unified part of this nature, but with the great gift and privilege to be carriers of the consciousness fractal. It is a very rare and beautiful identity to be the self, not the whole of consciousness but similar to it.

As you learned earlier, the chemical properties of each human's brain are privileged to be a fractal boson of consciousness, which is the jackpot win. Explain to your children the vast number of beings in nature who are conscious-less—and explain that this is the reason why humankind may develop, evolve, and expand forever until they become Supreme Beings.

You must give them this spiritual teaching, because their school education teaches them nothing about their true nature, nor the nature of consciousness. Despite this, you should teach your children to be sponges in school—be cautious, kind, and gentle. They should silently consider all of their teachers and fellow students to be the poor, innocent victims of the current world powers' governing system. Students and teachers are one and the same: victims.

Personally, I removed myself from school and educational institutions, and I am constantly self-taught. However, I only reached this point after decades of searching, fighting like a lion against demons, and evolving. Although school is a poor attempt at educating human beings, I would never ask parents to remove their children from school. That would be the ideal solution for their education, but it is too early for such a revolutionary action. Removing your children from schools is not advisable at this stage of evolution.

Instead, teach them the New Fundamental Life outside school. Give them the education they need to spiritually evolve. Moreover, teach your children to follow a simple, natural lifestyle with a simple, friendly, natural diet. Help them avoid the processed, unhealthy eating, smoking, and drinking culture of the current youth. They must treat their bodies as the vessel that will take them through this life.

With patience and care, you must start teaching the fundamental principles to your children as your highest personal spiritual goal. Observe your children practicing the five fundamental principles and starting to gain the fractals of trophies. Your children will enter the New Fundamental Life as proud, humble people perfectly equipped to become friends and shareholders of a new way of life.

Instead of football trophies, help them obtain the trophy that is the Spontaneous Forces, which are the Earthly applications of the conscious realms on Earth. Then help them attain the trophy of structural thinking, the trophies of collective observation and unified time, the trophy of the creation the past, and the trophy of neutralisation.

Then, you will have fulfilled your duty in style. You will feel like a true composer, and you will know that you have created a beautiful past for your children. You, of course, are already in the area of the New Fundamental Life and ready to participate in the evolutionary race of intelligence, ready to move forward forever until you join the conscious realms and become a Supreme Being.

Lovingly creating our own past

First, I must remind you what "love" means for me. Never forget the new meaning of love: knowledge, passion, and enthusiasm to learn, gain new power, abolish the old and adopt the new, evolve, and always move forward.

If you do not have children, or if your parents have violently created your past, it is still possible to lovingly create your past from here onwards. Remember that it is never too late to start on a new path for those who are willing to embrace a new perspective.

The common person uneducated in spiritual experiences sees the world from their eye to their nose. They deal exclusively with moderation in the context of obedience and adaptation to a desperately small field of space. They live in the present as if they are unique. Not with the perception of a mystic of eternity, but with the perception of a puppy who does not know everything they see and does not understand everything that happens to them. They inevitably end up crashing into something.

The feeling of injustice, of failure, of " I deserved something better" is very common among ordinary people. Everyone carries the nostalgia—but also the burden—that they have wasted their time. Everyone believes that the times were not with them, that they were not advantageous or "lucky" enough to achieve something more. They believe that entropy stole their opportunities for success in life.

Ordinary people are unaware that the sole culprit of their personal failure is themselves. They are the one who has wasted their own time in the mortal realm by carrying out the commands of those in authority or being entertained by the methods imposed on them by the respective authority. Thus, entropy takes them.

You, as a shareholder in the Spontaneous Forces, may now bypass the law of entropy. The previous management of chemicals in your brain made a burden of consciousness instead of a blessing. But as explained before, consciousness is not governed by anthropic laws, so you may bypass such laws if you know how to.

To do so, you must intensively prepare to maintain your mental energy with a boundless supply of novelty and inspiration. By practicing your daily communication with the Supreme Beings, and with the passing of the decades, you will discover many new concepts through the Spontaneous Forces that will make you wise and keep your mind fresh, eliminating any entropy in your brain and mental activity.

With this new knowledge, over the years, instead of your brain ageing and rotting, it will become more fresh and dynamic, with greater capacity and ability to absorb more powerful knowledge. Your mind will become the most powerful tool you possess. As a result, not only will you experience no loss of energy with human ageing, but your energy potential will constantly increase, leaving scientists screaming over your ability to seemingly bypass the law of entropy.

The last step before escaping

We have talked about achieving small feats, but you must also achieve the great feat, which is the last step before you may escape your fate: **aggressive meditation**. This form of meditation is totally different from the daily form of communicating with the Supreme Beings, which is kind, peaceful, and calm. This type of meditation is your active communication with the world we live in, and the battles and wars against this current world. Aggressive meditation means war—but this is not a war with weapons. It is a war of spiritual doubt and the rejection of established standards that chain your mind and being.

In this concept of meditation, the mentality of the practitioner is the exact opposite of when they are communicating with the Supreme Beings. In the gentle form of communication described earlier, the practitioner looks up at the Supreme Beings with calmness and kindness. The practitioner acknowledges their lower position in the mortal realms, and they look up to these higher beings. They look up from below.

With aggressive meditation, there is no place for calm and kindness. The practitioner is between the conscious realms and the mortal realms, and so they are elevated above their former position on Earth. They look down on the rest of humanity, who are now below them. They look down from above.

Note that this is different from the bottom-up method of self-learning; that is about education, while this is about perspective and developing the way you view the world. At the moment, your view of the world is limited to the space between your eyes and your nose. With each step you take, you become aware of your previous step. So, you must remain open-minded on your journey and develop your view of the world through aggressive meditation.

For example, every morning I watch Sky News to study the current media's poor usage of the English language. I watch the presenter journalists of the British media, who get sky-high salaries not to present the news but to act out whatever they are told to. Like football stars, they are merely entertainers. In aggressive meditation, I look down from my position above the screen to see such foolishness.

Aggressive meditation is therefore the self-certification that the world without me is doomed to collapse, while with me, there is a hope of survival, although it will be challenging. We must defend the hope of survival through aggressive meditation against this chaotic world that we live in. In my case, before publishing this book, the world was ignorant of my existence, so it was without me. But with the emergence of *The Temple*, the world is with me. *The Temple* is my aggressive meditation against this chaotic world.

In your case, dear friend, you can apply aggressive meditation in your own cosmos. Please do not compare your cosmos with anybody else's or with my own. It is different for each of us. For me, being able to view the world from above, from outside, is one of the rare qualities of the Aspergian brain. Yet, this sense became stronger because I exercised it to develop it to the highest level.

Of course, it takes time to develop this view of humanity, but you may start with a simple example. In the global weather forecast, I see the map of the planet from above, and I say to myself "Hey, I am now in the position of the Supreme Beings watching the planet from above to below." In aggressive meditation, you look at the world from up to down—the opposite of when you communicate with the Supreme Beings—and this takes practice.

With time and practice in looking from up to down, the practitioners of aggressive meditation have the urge for revenge and punishment against those who harm them and their planet. They have an urge to set the order for a superior way of living for humanity. This is why aggressive meditation is war. The spiritual battles in this war will be fierce and long-lasting, and you cannot win them without being the Hercules of spiritual powers.

Yet, when you achieve this new sense, it is so strong that you feel like a superhuman. You feel intensely that there is no human being who can stand against you. Your contemplation removes all of the asinine theories, claims, and proofs of other humans. Yet, having achieved the neutralisation of emotions, you feel no bitterness about their beliefs.

Instead, you will be rewarded with creative peace, which marks your final detachment from the animal kingdom and the beings that were your fellow humans. Your prize as the winner of this spiritual war is basking in the creative peace you receive.

Creative peace is the phase of peace that follows victory in the spiritual wars against the chaotic and unfair world that is heading quickly towards self-destruction. However, the publication of this book is a big victory, and my brain may now enjoy creative peace. This is a phase of constructive mentality and pure, neutral emotions— neutralisation as I explained earlier.

In this state, my brain is armed with the anger and motivation to secure peace against the demons who rule the world and lead it towards catastrophe. So, creative peace is full of brain activities and brain creations after victory, and it is a necessary step to prepare myself for new and bigger victories until the end of the battles against these demons.

If this sounds surprising to you, then you must understand that there is no peace without war. This is an essential duality. In fact, dualities are one of the main sub-forces of nature. Light and darkness, fairness and unfairness, peace and war, and so on. The paradigms of dualities are vast, and they govern your basic ideas of being.

In this book, you have seen the dualities of the pair universes—the material and the conscious universe. From this duality arises our pair of natures as human beings—the material nature and the conscious nature, and the Goldilocks Zone before and the universal law of fairness after.

However, the prize of creative peace is not the end of the road. Instead, it is the beginning of the road to a new field of perception and consciousness. You are now a new form of intelligence, detached from your fellow animals and humans. You may even make the diagnosis that most humans and animals are effectively one and the same. You are spontaneously self-confident, and the escape is then complete.

You will wake up every morning full of energy and confidence. You will always be in creative peace. You will hear people's stories and complaints, like "stress is killing me", and you will feel sorry for their misery. With a shining mind, a blossoming light on your face, endless spiritual well-being, and full health, you will be ready to lovingly create your past and the past of your children, if you have them.

Being is existing

Understand that zero does not eliminate one. We exist now, we can exist afterwards, and we can exist forever. I know this, and my spontaneous self-confidence in my knowledge is not up for discussion. Nor do I care to convince anyone about it.

This knowledge is my investment in the next phase of my evolutionary course. You too have the opportunity to gain new knowledge, superior to what you have learned in the whole of your previous life before this book appeared. Even if your share of this new knowledge is very small, it is sufficient to re-invent your plan of creating the past, discover your own position in this world, and understand your mission in this plan.

The doctrine of my teaching on the creation of the past is the strong conviction that the evolutionary course is without borders, limits, and barriers (such as physical death). In the context of this doctrine, eternity without an end to our evolution means that the transfer of information is absolutely possible. Information is not trapped in a given space and is not cut off by mortality.

Moreover, as the conscious entity who is the controller of your brain, *you* determine the content of the information that is stored there to be transferred in your post-Earth life. So, you create your own post-Earth life; you create the past of your current entity.

Do not let chance and randomness rule you and decide for you; do not allow them to take you backwards instead of forwards. Do not deny yourself eternal evolution, because you will be forced to violently retreat into extreme conditions of misery, like a lost child on the streets of a big city, a soldier on the front line, a slave, a prostitute, a prisoner, or a destitute labourer.

If you feel doubt at any point on your journey, always keep in mind that everything continues. There was no beginning, and there is no end. The same universe of matter is born and reborn forever; it is born everywhere but not somewhere as explained earlier, and it expands elsewhere forever in perpetuity until it is reborn. There are no such things as "nothing" or "nowhere". Remember that the universe was born spontaneously everywhere, because there is no logical specific point in space-time to be described as "somewhere" because space-time did not exist anywhere before the Genesis.

The content of this book is in the context of the command. We know where we are now, we know the properties of the host universe, and we know the neutral flow of time. We know the true nature of consciousness, and we know the next stage of transition—

evolution—to the universe of evolving matter. With this knowledge, we can create our past, applying the five fundamental principles to our lives, gazing at the higher plains from the top of the great Egyptian Pyramids, equipped with our trophies, our shield, and our compass.

Now, you see the path, the passageway between the torn sea. It is the narrow path free from stupidity, pettiness, greed, innocence, ideologies, established standards, religions, and idols. Oh, narrowly adorned path, how much I love that you lead me to the new plateau of the new perception of the new world to come. The new world is coming. Goodbye to this one with peace and harmony.

What else I should say other than:

Welcome to the New Fundamental Life.

Welcome to the evolutionary way.

Conclusion

BENEDICTION

Understanding your nature, origin, destiny, and destination is of crucial importance in your life. Now that you understand these things, you have two options in front of you:

1. Eternal, never-ending evolution.
2. Belief in non-evolution and eternal non-existence.

It is your choice whether you decide to be a winner in the cosmic plans and evolve to reach the conscious realms—or cycle through the mortal realms when your life here on Earth ends, on an endless treadmill of misery.

If you choose not to take the path of evolution, the consequence is self-abandonment to the mercy of cruel chance, where others decide your destiny. You will be erased from the annals of time, identified with nothing.

For those who have decided they are part of the cosmic plans, this book, *The Temple*, is an unprecedented fermion of powerful, new knowledge. Even if you are not sufficiently trained or adequately equipped for the journey, you are on the right path. The search for the conscious realms of existence and consciousness is constant and arduous, but it offers energy, light, and brilliance in every moment of your life.

The reward—one of many—is the negation of cruel chance on your path. This is the greatest spiritual reward for any traveller in the mortal realms. It is obtained by determining for oneself that one's course is that of evolution, of *ever forward*.

If you manage to attain even a small percentage of the shares of higher knowledge, then you will be a winner. You do not have to be ambitious about your shares. Even a very small percentage is enough for a great transformation to occur, for you to reinvent your life.

You should always know that you are at the beginning. Not at the starting point, but at the beginning of a new life. You have the privilege of re-inventing your life and creating a better past. To take part in the long-awaited evolutionary race of intelligence, you need to make a titanic effort in applying the fundamental principles, and you must hold firm your shield of patience and compass of logic. It takes courage, dedication, and constant study and engagement to evolve. But even if it requires you to fight for two or three universes, that should not bother you because from the moment you choose evolution, each new appearance in other mortal realms is a step forward.

Of course, you will also experience immediate gains. First off, you will instantly understand that the scientists and the faithful of various churches do not differ, even if it seems that they are arguing about who has the most truth. Both groups live in a capsule of illusion. On the one hand, scientists absolutely and unreservedly believe they are nothing more than molecules of matter. On the other hand, the faithful live in anticipation of the righteous salvation of the mind, following the commandments of some judge-god who will decide whether they see the light after death or are cast into outer darkness. Maybe they will end up in an intermediate phase, a grey area!

The second gain, an immediate benefit even from the first day of reading, is awareness and a change in the way you perceive the world and the humans in it. From now on, you will know why so many people suffer so greatly. You will know how to escape such suffering, and you do not have to repeat those sufferings. You do not need to squander your life without the slightest gain, without the slightest move in the direction of evolution.

You will see how those in the Dark Rooms have infiltrated every element of human life, filling your minutes and hours with endless work, debt, and idolatry until there is no time for you to notice what is really happening here. You will be free from such idolatry, from debt, from failed governance, and the bankrupt democratic state. You will be free from the tools of tyranny wielded by the barons in the Dark Rooms.

You and I will be on the side of all the wronged and innocent, and of those who decided to evolve. You will be against violence, and also against any attempt to exercise violence against you. You will want to live in a peaceful, peace-able, and law-abiding state made up of citizens who respect the law and put public interest above personal, private interests. Being against violence, however, means you will apply the new ruthless, merciless form of intelligence against those who do not obey the laws of peace and harmony.

Your third gain is the awareness of physical time and understanding of unified time, where all of your moments are connected and you can create your past, lovingly. You will not tremble at the fleeting nature of moments, for all of your moments are woven together in a beautiful tapestry of life. You will not fear illness, ageing, or your mortal death.

The choice of evolution means very simply that you will continue. You will not end with the end of the death of your physical body. As a conscious being, you will leave this planet for the next phase of evolution, which cannot be reversed. You will rise to a new level because you chose it. Anything that follows will be better than here and now. You have abolished the violent oppression of brutal chance. You have ruled out the possibility of appearing in any other mortal realm under similar or worse conditions than the present ones.

You will be a member of a group of privileged people who have immersed themselves in the font of this knowledge, and you will be great and strong in your peculiar humility. Your brilliance will emanate from the top of the world—and you will be its light. You will always be above those who have no training in spiritual experiences and no access to the applications of the fundamental principles, though you will be humble and loving in this knowledge.

You have seen the two possible directions. It is forward and backward. It is not right and left as presented in the scriptures of several religions, where right is the space of righteousness and good, and left is the space of the unrighteous, the sinner, and evil. Or right and left like in politics. It is forward or backward.

[189]

Your choice applies regardless of what happens to this planet. If your choice is forward, then it matters not if and when the Earth eventually self-destructs. Let the other Earthlings decide what they want. I hope they will keep the planet sustainable and hospitable for the development of intelligent life, for the training of consciousness, but it is not my choice.

I have done my duty in conveying this message to the world by offering *The Temple*, and I hope that you will join me in moving forward. If you do, we will live in glory with our great trophies, both on Earth in our mortal life and after the death of our mortal bodies—not as some arbitrary religious promise, but as shareholders in the Spontaneous Forces of the universe. Farewell my friend, who has chosen the way forward—the Temple—which means evolution.

OUR COMPOSERS

The Author: Noah Agrotes – Limassol, Cyprus

The sum of the stories of Noah's life is what you find in *The Temple*. All other events and details that do not contribute have been deleted as if they never happened. Noah was born in 1962, and he appeared in the right era, because he could not have appeared any earlier. No writer of this kind could have appeared at any other time in history in the 4.5 billion years of life on planet Earth. Noah's entire life before *The Temple* was a period of sacrifice and preparation for this purpose. From now on, he will live in the Goldilocks zone, the hospitable period for the development of his writing life. Neither earlier nor later.

Noah lives in Limassol, South Cyprus. He chose to stay on the island because he likes the climate there, except for the very hot summers, which he copes with much more easily and peacefully than he would if facing a harsh winter in the northern countries. He considers the Eastern Mediterranean region to be the most exciting place for someone to live. It is the area of the Magnetic Arc, extending from Western and Southern Turkey to Cyprus, from Egypt to the Middle East. This location enables great spiritual accomplishments.

However, Noah does not identify with the cultural attitudes and perceptions manifested on the island. He considers himself a foreigner there, especially after Al Jazeera disclosed the "Cyprus Papers" to the public, concerning the huge corruption in the government of South Cyprus. Noah has no relation to the corrupted government of the south. Indeed, he is an enemy of political corruption as one of his core principles. One of his personal goals is to contribute to the effort for political normalisation on a divided island. He is an absolute foreigner, as a foreigner is in every country in the world. A stranger here, a stranger everywhere.

One of Noah's goals in writing *The Temple* was to acquire personal spiritual gains, and he earned great treasures of higher, powerful knowledge on his path towards the metaphorical Ithaca. The journey to Ithaca was full of sighs, surprises, and anxious quests. It was a journey both on the surface and in the depths of the oceans of spiritual well-being and enjoyment. Noah's quest will continue in future books.

You can contact him at noahagrotes@yahoo.com

The Editor: Ameesha Green – Birmingham, UK

Ameesha was a discovery and a revelation. As you know, I tried dozens of editors before I found her, and I am proud of this amazing discovery! I believe that my editor was the compass needed to navigate the sea before I reached the shores of Ithaca. Without my wonderful and amazing compass, I would have been lost in the storms of erratic writing. Words, sentences, and paragraphs were the material from which this literary boat was made. The author was the helmsman, and the editor was the compass. Bravo Ameesha, my wise night-bird!

The Supporter: Sunday Michael – Nicosia, Cyprus

My sister Sunday offered her unwavering support during the exciting times and huge efforts of composing this book. She was awesome, pushing me to continue in her courageous way. She constantly insisted that "Any book is the author's personality, the author's pool of genes. You as the author, you are the pool of your genes." Bravo Sunday!

The Chef: Navjot Kumari, the Great Joti – Jalandhar, India

Joti is the miracle that came about in my life. There is no one else like her when it comes to care and devotion. She is proof of the light of the world. She is the only person whose portrait is included in this book as a dedication to her care for me.

The English Language Consultants:
Joseph Heber James – Phoenix, Arizona, USA and
Maxwell Forsey – Provo, Utah, USA

These two students contributed greatly to the competency and quality of English language in *The Temple*. Joseph is a student of mathematics; Maxwell of philosophy. Their contribution to this book is invaluable and priceless. I characterize the language of *The Temple* as philosophical and mathematical, owing to my two language consultants, whom I thank from the bottom of my heart.

Joseph is an exceptionally talented mathematician, and we can expect a lot from him in the field of mathematics in the years to come. As well as being a mathematical genius, he is fluent in foreign languages such as Greek and Japanese. I am privileged that this young genius worked hard on the language level of *The Temple*.

In addition to philosophy, Maxwell studies ancient cultures in the Mediterranean region. He is a systematic scholar of ancient civilizations and has previously translated texts from Ancient Greek and Latin. He studies these ancient languages and cultures in order to better understand the founding Western principles concerning government, religion, and the pursuit of happiness.

The Proofreader: Shaun Hand – Birmingham, UK

The Cover Designer: Nick Smith – Birmingham, UK

The Layout Designer: Kyle Albuquerque – Mumbai, India

The Web UX/UI Designer: Michele Tinnirello – Birmingham, UK

The Video Editor: David, ExplainerAds — Romania

The Marketers:
Elena Nazarova, Russian TV World — Limassol, Cyprus

Simran Bhogal — Birmingham, UK

Thank you and so long,
Noah Agrotes
Limassol, 2021

REFERENCES

1. Hugo Lagercrantz and Jean-Pierre Changeux, *The Emergence of Human Consciousness: From Fetal to Neonatal Life* (2009) in *Pediatric Research* volume 65, pages 255–260

2. Planets.org, https://theplanets.org/how-long-have-humans-been-on-earth/ (2020)

3. Bridget Alex, Discover Magazine, *How Did Human Language Evolve? Scientists Still Don't Know* (2018)

4. Roland Berger statistics on Consultancy.uk, *97% of population growth to be in developing world* (2015)

5. Tom Shingler, *Hot stuff: talking Tabasco with Took Osborn* (2016)

6. Statista.com, *Global unemployment rate from 2010 to 2020* (2020)

7. Harry Kretchmer, World Economic Forum, *How coronavirus has hit employment in G7 economies* (2020)

8. Andrea Peer, Worldvision.org, *Global poverty: Facts, FAQs, and how to help* (2020)

9. Larry Elliott, The Guardian, *World's 26 richest people own as much as poorest 50%, says Oxfam* (2019)

10. Dylan Matthews, Vox.com, *Want to stay out of prison? Choose rich parents* (2018)

11. Anneken Tappe, CNN Business, *The world is drowning in debt* (2020)

12. Troy Adkins, Investopedia, *What the National Debt Means to You* (2020)

13. SOS Children's Charity, Canada *Poverty in India: Facts and Figures on the Daily Struggle for Survival* (2020)

14. Statista.com *Number of smartphone users worldwide from 2016 to 2021* (2019)

15. Ofcom, *A decade of digital dependency (*2018)

16. Statista.com, *Number of social network users worldwide from 2017 to 2025 (*2020)

17. Pew Research Centre, *Teens, Social Media & Technology 2018,* July 2018)

18. Joshua Reiss, The Wire, *And So, All Pop Singers Sound the Same* (2016)

19. Tom Barnes, Mic.com, *Scientists Just Discovered Why All Pop Music Sounds Exactly the Same* (2015)

20. WebMD, *Porn Addiction* (2020)

21. Jessica Brown, BBC, *Is porn harmful? The evidence, the myths and the unknowns* (2017)

22. Fight the New Drug, *Let's Talk About Porn. Is It As Harmless As Society Says It Is?* (2019)

23. David Folkenflik, NPR, *The Bottom Line: Murdoch's Influence In The U.K.* (2011)

24. Hugh Gusterston, Sapiens.org, *What's Wrong With "the Chinese Virus"?* (2020)

25. Jim Waterson, The Guardian, *Most UK news coverage of Muslims is negative, major study finds* (2019)

26. Markham Heid, Time Magazine, *Is It Bad for You to Read the News Constantly?* (2020)

27. Amanda MacMillan, Health.com, *7 Ways Debt Is Bad for Your Health* (2019)

28. P. Arestis, M. Sawyer (editors), *Fiscal and Debt Policies for the Future,* Springer, (2014), Section 1.2: "Technocratic debt and deficit policymaking"

29. Robert A. Lavine Ph.D., Psychology Today, *Did Einstein Show Asperger's Traits?* (2016)

30. Ivan Couronne and Issam Ahmed, Phys.org, *Top cosmologist's lonely battle against 'Big Bang' theory* (2019)

31. Renata Micha, RD, PhD; Jose L. Peñalvo, PhD; Frederick Cudhea, PhD; et al, JAMA, *Association Between Dietary Factors and Mortality From Heart Disease, Stroke, and Type 2 Diabetes in the United States* (2017)

32. https://www.bytestart.co.uk/start-up-hit-1m-turnover.html

33. Michael Deane, 2020 "Top 6 Reasons New Businesses Fail", Investopedia (https://www.investopedia.com/financial-edge/1010/top-6-reasons-new-businesses-fail.aspx)